What people are saying about
Finding Your Moxie

D0711065

WOW!!! I could not put this down. _____ phenomenal. I love the way the stories are intertwined with the rest of the content. Every Woman will read this book and go, aha, I'm not the only person who feels this way and I can make a change if I choose to. Brilliantly written and definitely a page-turner.

~**Dr. Elaine Stevens,** CRS, Author & Relationship Expert, Founder - "The Relationship Wellness Center"

As a Residual Income Expert, Successful Network Marketer, and former Elite Trainer for over a decade with Robert Kiyosaki's "Rich Dad" Education Program, I find that in her new book, *Finding Your Moxie*, Debra Fox could not be <u>more spot on</u>! After reading the chapter "College and Knowledge Are Not the Same Thing," I am even more confident that the message is timely, insightful, factual and powerful.

~**Tracie Taylor,** Entrepreneur and Motivational Speaker

This terrific read actually provides new and valuable insights. I hope it inspires people to think outside the box and make a positive impact on the world around them.

~**Stacy Bandock**, 2015 Business Manager, Miss Rodeo America, Inc.

When faced with the tough situations of life, Debra Fox has the AMAZING ability to say and do what most people wished they'd said or done—with dignity! *Finding Your Moxie* is a **must have** for anyone who is desiring to kick life's myths and lies to the curb. Not only will Debra dust you off and get you back up on your feet, she'll inspire you to live your life to the fullest.

~**Dawn Jones,** Bestselling iTunes Author
of Top *7 Personality Challenges*

Debra Fox is a force to be reckoned with, and she doesn't beat around the bush. *Finding Your Moxie* is a complete eye-opener for women trying to thrive in love and life, but struggling to keep up with the myths and lies surrounding success. In one easy read, **Debra will teach you to stop playing by everyone else's rules, and become your own success story.**

~**Courtney Morris,** LA Television Casting Producer

Debra Fox has a communication style that manages to smack you upside the head while giving you a great big hug. She's the coach in your corner that you've always wanted. And needed. This gal has lived it all—and now she tells it all.

~**Jan Harrison,** Chief Solutions Officer with
JHarrison Solutions; Former Executive with a
Major Healthcare Firm; Broadcast Journalist

Finding Your Moxie

Finding Your Moxie

Myths and Lies Successful Women Kick to the Curb

DEBRA FOX

Made for Success
PUBLISHING

Made For Success Publishing
P.O. Box 1775 Issaquah, WA 98027
www.MadeForSuccessPublishing.com

Copyright © 2016 Image Development Group, Inc.

All rights reserved.

In accordance with the U.S. Copyright Act of 1976, the scanning, uploading, and electronic sharing of any part of this book without the permission of the publisher constitutes unlawful piracy and theft of the author's intellectual property. If you would like to use material from the book (other than for review purposes), prior written permission must be obtained by contacting the publisher at service@madeforsuccess.net.
Thank you for your support of the author's rights.

Distributed by Made For Success Publishing
Cover Design by DeeDee Heathman
Interior Design by DeeDee Heathman

Library of Congress Cataloging-in-Publication data
Fox, Debra
    Finding Your Moxie: Myths and Lies Successful Women Kick
    to the Curb
        p. cm.
        ISBN: 9781613398388
        LCCN: 2015920971

For further information contact Made For Success Publishing
+14255266480 or email service@madeforsuccess.net

Printed in the United States of America

CONTENTS

PREFACE

Over my lifetime I have been called a "bitch with balls" on more than one occasion. As far as I can remember, the comment was usually from men. As crass as that may sound to many, coming from men, I soon figured out it was usually meant to be a compliment.

I credit that attitude with my being able to achieve what I have in my life in spite of obstacles, and that attitude is the foundation of this book. Although I didn't feel that would be a good title for the book (primarily because women may view that as a negative thing), I wanted to express the same strength and attitude.

I chose the word Moxie for the title because I truly felt it represented me, the key to my success, my story, and my message. Some people may remember Moxie as one of the original soft drinks sold in the late 1920s. Today, Moxie has taken on another meaning.

Moxie {mok-see} (noun, American informal):
vigor; courage; know-how; spirit; aggressive energy; confidence; fearlessness; fortitude; determination; gumption, and just plain guts!

I've spent my life being told, "You're too fat," "You're not big enough (in your industry)," "You're not educated enough," "You're not successful enough," "You're not political enough," "You don't ass-kiss enough," "You're not nice enough," and on and on. I spent the early part of my life feeling like an outcast, defeated by the opinions of others, beat down and ready to give up. Quite frankly, it was EXHAUSTING!

If you have *Moxie*, you won't let any setback stop you from trying again, because you're a determined person who doesn't give up easily.

Finding Your Moxie is a no-nonsense, matter-of-fact, straightforward, realistic look at your life and how to develop enough Moxie to overcome, plow through, stand up for and achieve whatever it is you set as your goals in your life.

Every day in my seminar rooms, classes and speaking engagements, I look out at the faces of women who are beaten down and fed up. Many of them have been led to believe that because of one thing or another, they simply won't be able to reach their goals, achieve success or be happy. They spend the majority of their lives surrounded by well-meaning people, marketing firms and advertising agencies who are committed to selling them a false bill of goods in the form of myths, lies, and half-truths.

In order to be successful, you MUST have a college degree.

In order to be successful, you MUST have the perfect smile.

In order to be successful, you MUST make a lot of money.

In order to be successful, you MUST look like a model.

In order to be successful, you MUST...you MUST...you MUST!

I think you get the picture.

And like me, I find that many of them feel defeated and are either ready to give up, or worse yet, have already given up.

So they settle. They settle into a routine; they settle for a job instead of a career; they settle for a "second-hand" life, and they may even settle for a life partner who really isn't the best partner for them.

As a result of my upbringing and a change in the world around me, I was suddenly surrounded by a world that was telling me I didn't have what it was going to take to be successful. Even in the late 1970s and early 1980s the prejudices were still strong against women in the workplace.

That isn't where it stopped. I grew up watching Cinderella and Snow White and falling into what later became known as the Cinderella Complex: believing that my prince charming would find me and we would get married and live happily ever after. Unfortunately, like many, my first boyfriend in high school dumped me for one of my closest friends. I'm happy to say that they are still married today. At the time, however, I had just experienced my first in a long line of reality checks.

After receiving countless letters and emails, and having women approach me after seminars crying and telling me I changed their lives, I decided it was time to share my thoughts with the rest of the world.

Have you ever found yourself faced with reality checks? Have you had people tell you that you "can't be successful because..."? Have you given up, or are you ready to take the path less traveled and succeed?

If you said you are ready to take the path less traveled, then let's explore some of the more common myths and half-truths that I grew up with and share what it takes to be confident and successful in spite of them.

Moxie Minute:
BITCHOLOGY

I stand up for myself and my beliefs.
I stand up for those I love.
I speak my mind, think my own thoughts.
I won't compromise what's in my heart.
I live my own life MY way.
I won't allow anyone to step on me.
I refuse to tolerate injustice.
It means I have the courage and strength
to allow myself to be me.
So try to stomp on me, douse my inner flame or
squash every ounce of beauty I hold within.
You won't succeed.
And if that makes me a bitch, so be it.
I embrace the title and I'm proud to be a bitch!

INTRODUCTION

"If you're like me, you skip right over the Preface in a book.
If you did that, stop here, go back and read it."

The Author

I have found over the years, and still believe today, that our society places huge expectations and/or limitations on women regarding what it takes to be successful. First it was, "You have to have an undergraduate degree," then, "a master's degree is the new bachelors." We've now reached the point where you need a Ph.D. if you want to be considered competitive in the workplace. The magazines aren't much help either. "You need to be beautiful." Nope, "Now you need to be beautiful AND thin." And don't forget that your teeth need to be perfect and white, you have to have just the right tan, and you need to be able to schmooze people. Oh and don't forget, "You can be or do anything you want!"

Not only are there huge expectations or limitations placed on women regarding career successes, I believe there is another set of expectations placed on women...by other women. The difference between the two expectations creates a tightrope that women are expected to walk in order to keep everyone happy.

On a daily basis, you can receive countless pieces of advice that every person under the sun is willing to give you. These myths, lies and half-truths misrepresent what the true message *is* with well-meaning statements of what you *should* do instead.

Trying to figure out how to make your way through this crazy maze of expectations, both the ones placed on you by others and the self-inflicted unrealistic expectations we place on ourselves is a source of frustration for many.

But guess what? Being successful is not about keeping everyone else happy. It's about making sure at the end of each day that YOU are happy. It's taken me years, and tons of trial and error to figure out exactly how to do that. I'm going to share some cold, hard truths about the cold, hard truths — what it takes to achieve true inner happiness while still being successful.

Throughout my life, I have been blessed with so many wonderful and diverse experiences. But these experiences were only possible because of the choices I made starting at a very young age. While still in high school, I had the unbelievable opportunity to travel across the country performing with a semi-professional gospel group. Talk about learning how to get along with people in tight quarters. There were over twenty-five of us traveling on an old re-purposed Greyhound bus. We couldn't use the bathroom on the bus because the tuba was stored in the commode during our road trips! This is where I learned to sleep *anywhere* – including on the floor lulled to sleep by the humming of the transmission below me.

At age twenty, I competed for and was honored to win Miss Rodeo Kansas. For those of you who are unfamiliar with this program, this pageant selects a state queen to represent the PRCA (Professional Rodeo Cowboys Association). I spent the year traveling the state of Kansas promoting the professional sport of rodeo through appearances, radio and TV interviews, mall openings, hospital visits and more. This sounds wonderful until you realize that it was my second attempt at the title. My first year was a complete bust. I had to pick myself up, swallow my pride, regroup and start with a new plan to come back the second year. As a result of my commitment to my goal, I had the fantastic opportunity to represent Kansas in the Miss Rodeo America pageant.

As quirky as being Miss Rodeo Kansas may sound to some, I can without a doubt state that it was this experience that led me to the career path I'm on today. This is the experience that helped me regain much of the confidence I lost earlier in my life.

I worked as an account executive in the advertising industry and later became the director of New Faces for a mid-western based international modeling agency. While there, I took modeling classes and became a regional print and runway model. A few years later, I opened my own modeling and talent agency, joined the American Modeling Association and a year later was voted by my peers to serve two consecutive terms as the president of the association.

Over the years, I've started three businesses from scratch with absolutely no financial investment. Today I am an international corporate trainer and motivational speaker and have spent the last two decades speaking and conducting corporate seminars for the continuing education division of two universities. So what? Why is any of this special?

All of my success was achieved as a plus-size woman with not-so-perfect teeth, a very assertive personality and no formal degree. More importantly, I am happy, very happy! I live comfortably. I am financially independent (not reliant on a J.O.B. or a husband to pay my bills). Most importantly, I don't have to sit in a cubicle all day.

Between my parents telling me to "get a good job" and work there until I die, and numerous other naysayers over the years trying to tell me I couldn't be successful at what I wanted to do, I made it. Whew, thank goodness I didn't listen to all the naysayers, or I wouldn't be where I am today. And neither should you!

These experiences forced me to learn how to survive, how to take things with a grain of salt, how to stand up and dust myself off after being knocked on my rumpus, and how to be thankful for what I have been given. By default of all my experiences, I really have become a Jill of many trades. But I wouldn't trade one minute of my life. As a result of my life experiences, I have gained *endless* wisdom and common sense, which I draw on when needed. Not everyone can say that.

I now realize I have a very important message to share, but in order to understand how valuable this information is, you must first understand the hurdles and obstacles I've had to overcome to achieve my successes. I'm sure you will relate to many of them. They aren't major obstacles; no doubt there are other women who have experienced much worse and survived. However, they are the same obstacles that have emotionally crippled so many women from living their life to the fullest.

The successes I listed above are wonderful and I have been blessed. I'll be sharing more about these experiences throughout the book. But first, we have to go back to the beginning to understand the obstacles that could have negatively influenced my life.

Moxie Minute:

As I look back on my life,
I realize that every time I thought I was
being rejected from something good,
I was actually being redirected to something better.

CHAPTER 1

The Day I Was Born...

The day I was born, I was given a nickname that stayed with me for the rest of my life. Even today, after fifty plus years, my mother will still occasionally introduce me to people as her "little angel – her God-given miracle." No pressure, right!

Our family dynamic was not unusual for today, but in the mid-fifties, it was a new concept. My father fell in love with and married my mother and adopted my older sister (from my mother's first marriage) without hesitation. In 1954, my mother and father brought a new member into the family. Unfortunately, my brother died at twenty-three months of age to a congenital heart failure.

In the mid-1950s, a woman having a baby later in life was not encouraged. So after losing my brother, my older parents were encouraged not to have another baby. But alas, fate intervened, and two years later, exactly twenty-four hours after the birthdate of my deceased brother, I screamed my way into this world and was immediately given the nickname.

As a result of this nickname (and the constant reminder of it), I often felt like I was a replacement child and that I was expected to do great things. In another decade that probably would have been easier. But as a baby-boomer who was raised by older "veteran" parents, I became the victim of a changing world and was being guided by older parents who did not understand the changing opportunities and requirements for women.

Neither of my parents completed high school. In fact, both of them took their GEDs later in life. Nevertheless, even without a high school diploma, my father became a supervisor for a pipeline company. That was entirely possible in that decade. As a result, my parents did not understand the importance of my having a college education as we entered a new decade, and therefore they did not really plan for or encourage me to attend college.

Looking back I would say I was a "type A" kid…a classic over-achiever. I started my own business and was making money in second grade. Yes, you heard me right, in second grade. Clearly I started experiencing entrepreneurial tendencies at a very early age!

I consistently had a straight "A" average in school. At the ripe age of twelve, I was actively involved in our church Sunday school program, not as a participant, but as a leader and teacher.

Because I grew up on the back of a horse, my hobby as an early teen was riding and competing in horse shows. I learned early to work hard by taking care of my horses and equipment, and helping my father on the farm.

It was in the middle of my seventh-grade year that my father was transferred to Chatham, Illinois (south of Springfield) to take a supervisory position with his pipeline company. This was when my classic overachiever took a nose dive.

Being transplanted to a new school is always traumatic, but transferring mid-year was even more devastating. My new school had a very unusual way of assigning classrooms. Each grade had different class levels within the grade (i.e. 7A, 7B, 7C, 7D). So when I arrived, based on my "A" average, I was placed in the 7A class. Unfortunately, this school was more advanced than my previous school and I was not at the same learning curve. As a result, I completed my seventh-grade year with a straight D average. The next year I was moved to the 8D class. Talk about a slap in the face!

Now I was in a new school, had no friends, and was the laughing stock of my class because I was the new "stupid" kid. Do I even need to tell you what this did to my confidence and self-esteem? For the first time in my life, I began to experience insecurity. Like a brilliant flower taken out of its rich soil, I began to wilt.

The only escape from the loneliness was my horses. They became my confidants and closest friends, and I spent every free moment with them. It was the one place I retained any confidence and felt comforted. I would spend hours brushing, saddling and riding, all while crying and telling my horses how I felt about this move and how my life had been ruined.

In my thirteen-year-old desperation, I made the decision to write someone I really looked up to for advice on what to do. My hope was that he would be able to provide some sound suggestions, support and friendship that I was missing. I began drafting this all-important letter with great care, pouring my heart and soul out on vellum. I was sure this was the one person who would be able to help me make sense of it all.

One day in class, I was peeking at my handcrafted masterpiece when my teacher walked over to me. He took the letter off my desk and asked me what I was doing. Oh no, my confidante had been discovered. When I didn't reply to his question, he started reading my very private letter out loud to the class:

"Dear Donny..."

Even as I write this story, I cringe. I had written my heartfelt letter of desperation to Donny Osmond of the Osmond Brothers (for those of you who don't know, the Osmond Brothers were one of the original boy groups of our time along with the Jackson 5. Today it would be the equivalent of writing a letter to Harry with One Direction). Donny Osmond was my teen idol and I just knew that we would be married one day. So it only made sense that I would write to him for advice.

But now my private letter was thumbtacked to the bulletin board at the front of the classroom for everyone to see. Embarrassment and humiliation began setting in, and all I wanted to do was curl up and die. In addition to being the new stupid kid, I was now a big, fat, loser nerd too.

Right before we were transferred, my orthodontist announced that I would need braces. After the move and the embarrassment I had just endured, adding another level of humiliation like a mouth full of braces wasn't going to do me any favors. So I begged my parents relentlessly to forgo the braces.

Even though my mother should have done what was in my long-term best interest, watching her "God-given miracle" in so much misery was more than she could stand. She decided to give in. No braces for me! A decision I later painfully regretted.

Fast forward a few years. I entered high school, made some friends, was involved in the music department and had become involved with the church that sponsored the vocal touring group I mentioned earlier. I had survived my first major life crises and life didn't seem so bad. However, as high school began to come to a close, another set of challenges presented themselves.

As I mentioned earlier, my parents simply did not understand how the world was changing and what I was going to need to get ahead in my career choices. While many of my fellow high school students were being groomed for college, I was being taught that in order to get ahead in life, I had to work hard. "You trade an honest day's work for an honest day's wage," my father would tell me. In fact, I wasn't encouraged to take college preparatory classes in high school. Instead, during my senior year, I joined the work-study program and worked every afternoon as a secretary at the attached junior high school office.

My preparation for a career and life started with my first job in high school, rather than discussions of a college education. I even remember the day my mother sat down with me and said, "Your father is eligible for retirement now. If you go to college, he'll have to work another four years to pay for it." Guilt trip for one, please!

Looking back on those conversations, I would like to believe that had I told my parents I *wanted* to go to college, they would have made that happen. But as a seventeen-year-old who had a job, a boyfriend, was involved in a wonderful church, and was traveling and performing with a semi-professional gospel group, I really didn't *want* to go to college. Based on my upbringing and what I had been taught by my parents, I was already living the "American dream." Unfortunately, the American dream was about to take a hard left turn without me.

My father retired, and my parents planned to move from Illinois back to Kansas. I was quickly informed that I was not going to be permitted to stay in Illinois by myself, and since I was seventeen years old, I did not have the legal ability to do so. I was forced to give up my job, my boyfriend, my church and my singing group to move back to my birthplace. My parents, having lived there when I was born, called in favors and got me a new job without my knowledge, input or approval.

Although I started my "career" working as a secretary for the school district in Illinois and traveling across the country performing with a singing group, I suddenly found myself working in a library at an old Catholic school in small-town middle America.

That was the next chapter of my "career" whether I liked it or not.

It's right here that this story could take two different paths. I would either work at that library, or other entry-level/menial jobs for the rest of my life, or I could choose the path less traveled and do something my future self would thank me for later.

I came to the fork in that road and I...*I* chose the path less traveled.

What I learned in my life is:

You don't *need* a man.

You don't *need* wealth.

You don't *need* a degree.

You don't *need* a perfect body.

You don't *need* a genius IQ.

What you need is MOXIE!

Enough Moxie to overcome whatever life throws at you without wasting years and years feeling sorry for yourself.

Moxie Minute:

I didn't have the time, but I made time.

I didn't have the knowledge, but I did what I knew.

I didn't have the support, but I learned to support myself.

I didn't have the confidence, but the confidence came with results.

I had a lot going against me, but I had enough going for me.

I had plenty of excuses, but I chose not to use any of them.

CHAPTER 2

What is Success? The $64 Million Question

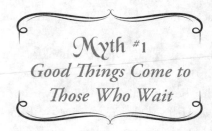

Myth #1
Good Things Come to Those Who Wait

Let's get things straight right up front: good things do NOT come to those who wait. Good things come to people who have Moxie! People who set goals, stay laser-beam focused on their goals, who don't internalize what other people say or think about them, and who work their butts off. Period.

When I started writing this book, I made contact with several of my long-term personal and professional friends – people who have known me the longest and watched me go through ups and downs. I posed this question to each of them:

"What characteristics or traits have you seen me exhibit over the years that you believe have helped me to achieve my success and/or happiness?"

I really had no idea what I would hear back, but I was interested in finding out. Did they see in me the same things I felt had helped me become successful?

One of my long-time female speaker friends said:

- You are always up for the confrontation, willing to battle for what you believe in
- Goal oriented
- Confidence in your skills
- Not concerned with being liked
- Proactive in dealing with situations
- Willing to learn and investigate

I wrote back and asked her, "Do you think these are positive traits?"

Her response was exactly what this book is about:

"Interesting question, because if you were a man, there wouldn't be a question of whether or not those traits are positive. Hell yes, they're positive — although other women probably don't see them that way."

The additional feedback I received was very similar. A long-term male friend shared this response:

- Passionate purpose: you are clear about what you intend to accomplish, and then plow through any obstacle to make it happen. Whether it's a short-term goal or a life goal... you believe!
- Perseverance: it takes perseverance to be successful. This is not limited to taking action. It has to include the perseverance of your vision and the inner knowledge that there is something you are moving towards. That success is deserved, available, and can be achieved.
- Visionary: being able to see through the complications of daily tasks and past life is a challenge. You appear to make a trail through the thickets of non-believers, skeptics, and rational thinkers seamlessly, even though it can be a full-time job all by itself. Of course, you can't always see the end result (that's up to a higher power many times), but you are a strategic thinker...you always have been. You see

beyond the here and now and see what could be. It's a true gift…doesn't always seem like a gift, but it is one.

- **Limitless:** when people set their own limits and boundaries, they remove the proverbial glass ceiling and likewise become limitless and without boundaries. I've always seen you as limitless and without boundaries. You've lived wherever you wanted to live…you've gone after any goal you wanted to go after…and you've never allowed others to set the boundaries for you.

- **Tenacity:** you have always had the *chutzpah* and audacity to move past the status quo of what an "uneducated woman from a meager upbringing" was capable of achieving (chutzpah — personal confidence or courage that allows someone to do or say things that may seem shocking to others.) I think these are traits that from the outside most people view as harsh and unyielding… but from the inside can be just as challenging to possess because pushing towards success isn't always pretty. Often these traits in a man's world earn "kudos." Unfortunately, in a women's world, these same traits might cause a woman to be labeled as a "bitch." You've never let this stop you.

Looking at all the input I received, what really resonated with me was a single comment that was consistent throughout every response I received. This comment alluded to the fact that men would be more likely to earn kudos or be considered normal and acceptable for having the traits I have, while a woman could easily be viewed as a bitch for having them.

Even more disheartening is the fact that the majority of the attacks on women exhibiting success traits are from other women. How very unfortunate that as a whole, women don't tend to support each other. Women take things personally, tend to be more sensitive, and make a lot of assumptions about successful women.

The sole reason I decided to write this book was to let women know that no matter what your background or history is, you CAN be successful. As I mentioned in the first chapter, I do not have a formal college education/degree. However, I have always been willing to learn. I research and study consistently. I have invested in myself by building my own educational library that I access often.

In addition, I've spent the majority of my life as a plus-size woman. No matter what people say, this does make a difference in how you are treated. If you are a plus-size woman, you better have a thick skin and be willing to go above and beyond in other areas to offset what society considers a "problem" or a sign of laziness.

I've always considered myself a go-getter, someone who can make a decision and act upon it without hesitation. I suppose I didn't realize that the traits my friends listed about me were in fact, traits. To me these characteristics were normal!

However, after reading the observations that my friends shared with me, I realized that while these are traits of successful people, not everyone exhibits these traits.

In following chapters, we will uncover and discuss success traits, as well as the myths we hear that negatively influence people.

Moxie Minute:

A real woman
~~has curves~~
~~is skinny~~
~~has muscles~~
is whatever the hell she wants to be!

THE DEFINITION OF SUCCESS

So where do we start when talking about how to be successful? With the definition of success, of course!

Success is…well, it's…let me think a minute.

Okay, now I have it. Success is…nope, lost it!

Well, that wasn't as easy as I had hoped. I have no problem telling you what success means to me but trying to provide a broader picture definition that applies to everyone is another story entirely.

Let's face it, the term "success" can be abstract at best. Given the fact that every single person could feasibly provide a different definition of what success means, trying to provide an across-the-board definition is like saying, "One size fits all."

So where do you start when you need to define something? The dictionary, of course! According to Merriam-Webster, the definition of success is:

- The fact of getting or achieving wealth, respect, or fame
- The correct or desired result of an attempt
- Someone or something that is successful: a person or thing that succeeds

Does that mean that success is only measured by achieving wealth, respect or fame? Well, for some people, yes. For some people their measure of success is to actually die with the most toys, and who are we to tell them their definition of success isn't right? There is no doubt that money can build a lot of things, solve a lot of problems, cure a lot of diseases, and fund countless positive organizations.

I just heard some of you screaming at me, "Money is the root of all evil. Jesus was so angry about money that he turned over the money changers' tables in the temple." For some religious people, this definition of success might be considered selfish and sinful.

Well, to be fair, the scriptures do not say that money is the root of all evil. The scriptures say that the LOVE of money is the root of all evil. Having money is not evil – how you got it, who you stepped on along the way, or what you do with it might be another story.

Let's face it, whether you want to die with the most toys or not, in today's world you most likely need money (yours or someone else's) to survive, so let's not be too quick to judge money as a negative thing. Have you ever heard the statement, "Money ain't everything"? Well, it may not be everything…but it's right up there with air! You simply can't survive in this world today without it.

But this chapter is about defining success, and if someone's goal is to die with the most toys and they do that, then by definition they have been successful.

To some people, success means winning at all cost. Competitive personalities see success as being the best or winning. This is a mentality that runs high in sports or pageants where just taking part and achieving good results is not enough. On the other hand, some people may be just as satisfied by simply trying and giving their best, whether they win or not.

Clearly success in life and/or career *should* mean different things to different people. To most people, however, success means achieving *something*: status, wealth, fulfilled life, winning awards, graduating top of the class, being the top sales person, winning a pageant, family…the list is endless.

In order to be successful at anything, you must first make a decision as to what you are trying to achieve. You know, set your goals — set the GPS for your life journey. This requires having a plan, and executing the plan.

I can hear the rumblings beginning! "I knew she was going to talk about setting goals. I'm so tired of people telling me to set goals. I don't believe in setting goals. I believe in taking life one day at a time and being the best at whatever life or God unfolds for me."

Really? First of all, I believe even God had goals. Don't you suppose God knew, before He ever waved his hand to create the heavens and the Earth, what His desired outcome was?

I had a man in one of my seminars say to me, "I don't set goals because I don't want to be disappointed. I like where I'm at. I go to work, I come home, I go bowling every Tuesday and I go to bed. I don't set goals."

I looked at him and asked, "So would it be fair to say that your desired outcome is to be happy with where you are right now and not create situations where you might be disappointed?" He answered, "Exactly!"

I smiled and said, "I don't know how to tell you this, but you just set a goal. You just created a destination. And if you are living exactly the way you just described, then you have been successful in achieving that."

The audience laughed, as did the participant who had challenged my theory. After the class was over, he stopped me and said, "I suppose now you're going to tell me that if I'm not happy where I'm at, it's because I didn't set any goals."

I said, "Nope. I'm going to tell you if you're not happy where you're at, it's because you set the wrong goal. You sat down in your life car, plugged the wrong destination into your life GPS and decided it's easier to stay on the wrong path than to have the GPS recalculate the correct destination."

A dear friend of mine, Jan Harrison, is an outstanding trainer and corporate consultant. Some years ago I had the pleasure of traveling with her for several months as we conducted a women's conference nationwide. During one of our sessions, Jan was talking about what motivates people to change. She referenced a phrase that we've all heard a million times, "Stuck between a rock and a hard place."

This old phrase refers to being in a desperate situation. History tells us that desperation can be a great motivator. If you are at the end of your rope, out of options, about to lose everything, or stuck between a rock and a hard place, you are more likely to say, "Something needs to change." You might actually be forced to turn your life around and do something different in order to get different results.

One day, however, I heard Jan say that many people don't make changes in their life because they are stuck between "a rock and a soft place." Now that was a new concept! She went on to explain that many times people will settle for where they are because even though it isn't what they originally wanted, or it wasn't their original "destination", they ARE comfortable. So they settle in and just live from day to day.

Imagine owning a couch that you've had for years, but one day a spring pops up in one of the cushions. How many of us would run right out and buy a new couch? My guess is very few. Most would either sit on the other end of the couch, or just turn the cushion over.

This is what we mean by "stuck between a rock and a soft place." Not ideal…it's comfortable; it's familiar; it's safe. And so we settle.

I find that people will often change their definition of success to match where they are, instead of changing where they are to reach their real definition of success. Why? The most obvious reason is because change is not easy or fun.

Regardless of what your definition of success is, there are some unfortunate kickbacks from reaching some destinations (i.e. the negativity from people who are envious of your success). If you are great at what you do, and you reap benefits that others are not willing to work for, jealousy may rear its ugly head and attack you.

Being a pageant coach in the rodeo queen world, I see this consistently. If someone wins besides THEIR daughter, it HAS to be rigged, political or a blatant example of favoritism. When parents start down this path, they teach their children to do the same. Nothing screams sore loser faster than someone screaming, "Rigged!"

Just to be fair, I have to say that in all situations, there is the remote possibility that it *was* rigged or political, or that you did get beat out by favoritism. However, yelling, "Foul!" rarely changes the situation, and quite frankly, makes you look bad.

Being successful usually includes being a gracious loser, being able to compliment others when they succeed, even when that is the last thing in the world you want to do.

On the flip side of the coin, when you are the winner or reach your destination and someone else yells, "Foul!" or attacks you, it can end up being bittersweet *unless* you have Moxie. You have to be a strong, confident individual not to internalize negative comments and *choose* to get your feelings hurt. When this happens it is imperative to remember and focus on the people in your life who DO support you, and celebrate your successes with you. I talk more about this in chapter ten, "Life is Like an Elevator."

If you choose to doubt yourself, another unfortunate thing can begin to happen. You can begin to succumb to insecurities and depression. While writing this chapter, the news of Robin Williams' death dominated the country. While considered one of the most successful comedians of my lifetime, his success did not compensate for the emptiness or darkness he suffered from. While successful at achieving his goals, at reaching his destination of achieving comedic fame, he was not successful at finding personal peace and satisfaction from his career success. This clearly confirms that career success does not always equal life success.

Does this suggest that for every person there may be two success paths we have to map out: one personal and one for our career? While I would certainly agree that they overlap, I believe that success in one does not automatically imply that you will be successful in the other.

Unfortunately, many people seem to believe that personal happiness is a by-product created by achieving success in their career, college, pageant or other types of goals. In reality, it may be imperative that you find personal happiness first. For example, it's very difficult to be happy with a life partner, if you can't be happy alone first. Career or life success can be short-lived and may not keep you personally happy.

Is your destination to be the CEO of a Fortune 100 company, or to be an extremely effective wife and mother? These seem like two very opposite goals. If two women individually achieve these goals, does that make one woman more successful than the other? Well, that is the $64 million dollar question!

In the example I gave earlier about the man in my seminar, many may instantly jump to the conclusion, "That guy is just lazy and has no desire to better himself." Depending on their definition of success, they might be correct.

However, if that guy was *truly happy* doing what he was doing, and not negatively affecting others, then I say he was successful at reaching his destination and achieving something. He IS successful.

If your goal is to be the best wife and mother on the planet, then DO IT!

If your goal is to be the CEO of a Fortune 100 company, then DO IT!

If your goal is something in between, then DO IT!

Regardless of what your success destination is, there are success characteristics that apply to all success journeys. Sitting around wishing for success is NOT a characteristic. You must select a destination, map your course, and then take action accordingly. Success does NOT come to those who wait. Success comes to those who take action.

The key point here is to acknowledge that you, and only you, have the power to decide what success means to you and as a result, you don't get to blame anyone else if you miss the mark.

What it all really boils down to is this. Are you truly happy where you are?

If your answer is no, then maybe it's time to reset your life GPS. Maybe it's time to ask yourself these questions:

- What is my true destination; what is it that will make me happy?
- Am I clear about where I'm going; what I'm trying to achieve?

OR,

- Did I settle?
- Did I give up on my goal/destination?
- Did I change my destination to fit where I ended up?

These questions require some real soul-searching. My dad called it, "having a come to Jesus meeting with yourself." Having to take an honest look at yourself and where you are in life. If you're not honest with yourself, you may continue down the wrong path.

So, now that we've uncovered the definition of success…

Wait. Have we uncovered a clear definition yet? It appears we have come full circle without a clear conclusion.

How about this quote from Maya Angelou:

"Success is liking you, liking what you do, and liking how you do it."

Or this quote from an unknown author:

"Your success is measured by the strength of your desire, the size of your dream, and how you handle disappointment along the way."

While there may not be one clear definition of success, I am pretty confident about what success is not. Success is not something that someone else can decide for you. It is not a goal that someone else can define or dictate for you.

As children, our parents can and should guide us by providing options, directions, examples and choices as it relates to our own personal future successes. By today's standards, that usually equates to providing children with post-secondary education opportunities. Unfortunately, college and knowledge are not the same things. We will explore this more in chapter nine.

In my case, my parents provided me with options of success based on what they knew, and that was based on the fact that neither one of them had a high school diploma. Had I not mastered self-education and a "never-give-up" mentality, I would not have been able to change my personal destination and goals.

Clearly, the definition of success can change. It changes from generation to generation, from person to person, from industry to industry. At the end of the day, however, the decision whether or not you are successful is completely up to you.

Maybe your success destination isn't so much about becoming anything. Maybe it's about un-becoming everything that isn't really you so you can be who you were meant to be in the first place.

I love this quote from Steve Jobs, founder of Apple:

"Your time is limited, so don't waste it living someone else's life. Don't be trapped by dogma – which is living with the results of other people's thinking. Don't let the noise of others' opinions drown out your own inner voice. And most important, have the courage to follow your heart and intuition."

YOUR MOXIE MISSION
(Should You Choose to Accept It)

1. Acknowledge that success does NOT come to those who wait. Success comes to those who set goals, make a plan and then take action!
2. Make sure YOU know what is important to you. Think about the things that truly make you happy or satisfied. Be honest with yourself.
3. Do some research to find out if there is something outside of your current environment, comfort zone, location, or job, that you might be interested in learning more about.
4. Spend some time really thinking about this question, "If time and money weren't an issue, what would I want to do?"
5. Once you have that answer, ask yourself this question, "What is it going to take for me to be successful at this?"
6. Be realistic with yourself. Do you have the skillsets and drive to reach this goal? OR, can you make a satisfactory living doing this? If the answer is yes, get to work and get laser-beam focused on your target. If the answer is no, this can be a hobby, past time or something you do because you love it and it makes your heart sing. But you will also want to research destinations that utilize your natural God-given strengths, talents and skills, as well as the training you have invested in.

CHAPTER 3

Rude is in the Eye of the Beholder

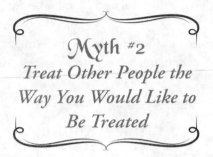

Myth #2
*Treat Other People the
Way You Would Like to
Be Treated*

A s we begin to venture into all of the myths, lies and half-truths that plague women today, we must first lay some groundwork that I will refer back to throughout the book. That brings us to Myth #2: *Treat other people the way you would like to be treated.*

No matter where I'm speaking or who the audience is, when I start this statement, the majority of the people in the audience will finish it. It's a common core lesson that we've all been taught, or at the very least have heard throughout our lifetimes.

In theory, it makes a tremendous amount of sense. "Treat people with respect because we all want to be treated with respect." So if we treat other people the way WE want to be treated, logic would tell us that we will be treated the same way in return. And that is where the conflict begins.

Every single day in my communication seminars, I talk about the roadblocks to being a confident and powerful communicator.

For over twenty years, I have trained on and discussed gender differences, lack of confidence, generational differences, lack of skillset, cultural differences, lack of preparation, and personality differences. Clearly, each one of these areas can create conflict or drive wedges between people and prevent them from being able to have calm, rational, respectful and effective communications with other people.

As we explore these roadblocks, we will discuss how they can create conflict or communication barriers for you.

Moxie Minute:

If you go through life believing that your generation, gender, culture or personality is the right way, the best way or the only way, you will automatically have conflict with a majority of the population.

GENDER DIFFERENCES

Do men and women communicate differently? That's probably one answer that men and women will agree on, and the answer is YES! This is not a new theory. John Gray brought the gender differences to light when he taught the whole world that *Men Are from*

Mars, Women Are from Venus. Quite frankly, that phenomenon has not changed over the decades.

These differences especially hold true when it comes to the way the genders communicate through conflict.

Take for example John and Bob, who are peers in a corporate environment. John delivers a presentation to the board of directors and right in the middle of it, Bob starts interrupting and pointing out errors in John's presentation. Of course, this puts John in a very embarrassing and uncomfortable position.

After the meeting is over, John stops by Bob's office to chat with him about how it went. "Bob, I really appreciated the thoughts you shared during the meeting. You made some valid points. I have to be honest and tell you that I didn't appreciate you sharing those points during my presentation and in front of the board. I do have a suggestion though: In the future, what would you say to getting together with a pot of coffee in my office, and going over presentations before the meeting so I can make the appropriate changes and corrections in advance?"

Bob's response? "Sure!"

Then John says, "Great. By the way, are we still on for golf Saturday morning?"

That's it! DONE! Issue addressed, solution presented and accepted, golf scheduled.

Now, I realize that each situation could vary. But the point I'm trying to make is this. For the most part, men address their concerns head on. They go directly to the person, express their concern and then when it's over they go play golf, get a beer, go to the races, or grab lunch.

I wish I could say the same about women, but alas, I cannot. When women have an issue with Bob, most women will talk to everyone about the issue EXCEPT Bob! As a result, we are viewed as a gossip or pot stirrer, and the chance of the issue being resolved is greatly diminished. To make matters worse, we won't let it go. We pass that grievance down through our lineage. Our great grand-children will know that we had a problem one time with this guy named Bob.

Interestingly, if a man thinks a woman is strong and direct, there is a high possibility that he will respect her for being able to assertively stand her ground. Predominantly speaking, however, if a woman assertively stands her ground with another woman, she will be labeled a bitch, and the cold shoulder routine will begin.

Too often we as women do not support each other through conflict or disagreement. We either avoid conflict, or we get defensive during conflict. Either way, we hold a grudge because we don't tend to address the conflict or listen and understand the other party. We rarely engage in conflict resolution.

Ladies, this inability to address issues directly with the one person who can do something about it could be costing you major credibility, advancement in your career and possibly even lost personal friendships and/or relationships.

We will discuss this issue in more depth in chapter seven, "Conflict is Not a Dirty Word."

GENERATIONAL DIFFERENCES

For the first time in history, this decade introduced the concept of four generations working side by side, where in past years we would only see three. At the writing of this book, those generations include the Veteran (or Silent) Generation, born 1934 to 1945; Baby Boomers, born 1946 to 1964; Generation X, born 1965 to 1980 and Generation Y, born 1981 to 2000. (Birth years vary depending on the research you access.)

In the United States, this change is due to a couple of key factors. First, the mandatory retirement age began to increase from sixty-five to seventy over a set period of time. Secondly, with the massive recession that took over the US in the mid to late 2000s, countless retirement eligible people lost their retirement funds and found themselves having to remain in the work force longer just to survive.

The different values, experiences, styles and activities of these four generations create misunderstandings, frustrations, conflicts and communication roadblocks.

In a *FORBES Magazine* article, written by staff writer Jenna Goudreau, she talked about her observation of how the generational differences impacted communication and created conflict in the workplace.

At a recent professional development retreat led by corporate trainer Dana Brownlee, a woman in her mid-50s stood up and starting citing a laundry list of communication conflicts on her mixed-age team. Chiefly, she was angry that the younger members rarely returned her phone calls by phone. Instead, seeing the issue as non-pressing, they typically would text or email back a response. The woman worked herself into such a frenzy that she suddenly spouted, "We need to stop emailing and pick up the %^$# phone!"

As she continued to speak, Brownlee realized the woman's concern ran deeper than mere frustration. Her voice cracked and her breathing faltered until she couldn't continue and sat down. It was more than anger. She felt disrespected and unappreciated.

Bottom line; when the "electronic communication" generations X and Y, treat the older workers the way they want to be treated, the Veterans and Baby Boomers may find it disrespectful and rude.

On the flip side, when the older generations (Veterans and Baby Boomers) treat generations X and Y the way they would like to be treated, the young workers find it condescending and rude.

Either way, both groups find it rude. In addition, both groups may even think the other group is wrong.

CULTURAL DIFFERENCES

Ah yes. Foreigners coming into our country, not speaking the language, and bringing all of their funny ways and religions with them!

Uh no, that's not what I'm talking about.

Over the past twenty years, I've had the pleasure of speaking and training in all fifty continental United States, Puerto Rico, Canada, Australia and New Zealand. As a result, I learned very quickly that while cultural differences certainly can refer to how people from different countries live and work, these differences can also be domestically within a country. For example, people in New York work and communicate VERY differently than people in the southern parts of the United States.

Here's a great example of how international cultural differences can be considered rude.

With a Starbucks or Dunkin' Donuts on every corner in the United States, people have access to every flavor of coffee under the sun. As a result, seminar companies stopped ordering coffee at seminars because the attendees would bring their own and the ordered coffee was just being poured down the drain. This is a rather costly waste.

During my first trip to train in Australia, it became quickly apparent that they take "tea time" very seriously. The seminar attendees there expect you to provide a fifteen to twenty-five-minute break so they can have a proper tea time, and you need to provide the coffee and tea. Usually, the hotels there have baristas that make each cup individually. This, big pot of generic coffee in the meeting room, was okay, but not preferred, and by golly you better have biscuits (cookies or pastries of some kind). In this culture, they find it terribly rude to host an event and not provide proper tea times. This is a great example of the title of this chapter..."Rude is in the Eye of the Beholder."

Every person, based on where they are born and raised, will have different cultural beliefs. These beliefs can be work related, religion based, dictate the speed at which they function and determine how accepting they are of other people.

These differences directly impact how we are willing to listen to and engage with other people, how accepting we are of their life choices, and how tolerant we are of the lifestyles of others as we are forced to work with them side by side.

Unfortunately cultural differences, the differences as viewed from both perspectives, creates conflict and communication barriers.

PERSONALITY DIFFERENCES

I am a firm believer that personality differences cause the greatest number of conflicts and communication breakdowns in both our personal and professional lives today. In fact, I tell seminar attendees and managers daily that if they are involved in a conflict, or manage two people on their team engaged in conflict, the first thing to look at is personality differences.

While there are numerous personality profiling systems dating all the way back to astrology, I would venture to say that the Myers-Briggs Type Indicator (MBTI) is probably considered the most used and recognized. The MBTI is an assessment tool that measures psychological preferences in how people perceive the world and make decisions. While very detailed, it isn't always user-friendly for the average Jane trying to understand, manage or avoid personality conflicts.

One of the other more common profiles is the DISC Model, which describes the four basic temperament types of human behavior as first introduced by Hippocrates 400 years before Christ: (Choleric) D-type, (Sanguine) I-type, (Phlegmatic) S-type, and (Melancholy) C-type. The DISC model measures only two dimensions of personality:

1.   A preference towards working with a task versus working with people
2.   An orientation towards being passive or being active

Quite frankly, the results of each personality profile will tell you the same basic information. There are four overall personality types. Each individual will exhibit characteristics in one of the four personalities more predominately than the other three. This does not mean that you exhibit ALL the characteristics of a single personality, just that you predominately lean into one quadrant. In addition, every person draws strengths and exhibits characteristics from their "sideline" personalities. This means that every person exhibits personality traits from three personality styles, one more predominately than the other two.

Personality profiling is not a new concept. For decades, corporations, organizations and counselors have had people take personality profiles and have had them trained on who they are and what makes them tick. In fact, most people reading this book have taken a profile before (or two or three). You most likely know who you are, what you like and don't like, and what it is that other people do that irritates you.

When I train on personalities in my seminars, I focus instead on how to use personality profiling to better communicate with other people, how to figure out who you are dealing with in your life (personality-wise) and how to talk their language. Here's what I mean.

If you lived in Germany, you would most likely speak German as your primary language. If you visited Rome for a vacation, their primary language would be Italian (for the sake of this analogy, let's assume those are the only two languages involved). If you live in Germany, and you decide to take a three-week vacation to Rome, there is a high probability that you would have trouble finding or getting the things you wanted or needed on your trip.

If you knew you were going to a country where you could not speak the language, and they did not speak your language, would you do one or more of the following?

1. Buy a translation guide and take it with you
2. Learn enough of the language to ask the important questions
3. Find an app for that

If you are like the majority of people who attend my seminars, you immediately said, "YES, I would do one or more of those things!" Why? Common sense…no one wants to go somewhere and not be able to get what they want or need, so most people would figure out how to communicate in a different way to achieve their desired results.

Dealing with different genders, generations and especially personalities is the exact same way. Every single individual, based on their upbringing, gender or personality type, will communicate, work, and process differently, and will likewise have different expectations.

When I talk about personalities in my seminars, I use animals to explain these differences. Let's take a look at that chart:

HIGH NEED TO DIRECT/OUTSPOKEN

P
E
O
P
L
E

T
A
S
K

LOW NEED TO DIRECT/INTROVERT

Every single day you cross paths with people and every single person you cross paths with is different than you in the way they think, how they process, what is important to them, what irritates them, and how they communicate.

So how can you possibly communicate better with another "animal" if you first don't know how to identify the animal you are dealing with? You can't! So, the first thing we have to do is learn how to identify people and learn who they are.

On the left side of the animal chart, you'll see the Peacocks and Lambs.

These two personalities are people/relationship driven. They LOVE people. They love to work with people, hang out with people, nurture people, go to lunch with people, and entertain people in their home. People, people, people! In fact, the Peacocks and Lambs are most likely the ones who come to work every morning, get a cup of coffee, walk up and down the

48

halls saying good morning to everyone and chatting about what they did over the weekend.

If you are that person, please note, you are driving the Lions and Owls out of their ever-loving minds!

On the right side of the chart, you'll see the Lions and Owls. These two personalities are task-driven. They are motivated more by budgets, projects, agendas, deadlines, lists, charts, graphs, details and use and misuse of time. They are extremely detailed in their processes and work methods.

The Lions and Owls are simply NOT the warm and fuzzy folks. Now don't misunderstand. I didn't say they aren't nice. They're just nice in a different way, which usually does not include all the over-the-top warm and fuzzy niceties that you might experience when dealing with the Peacocks and Lambs.

On the top of the chart you will find the Peacocks and Lions. These two personalities have a high need to direct and are more outspoken in their communication styles. What this means is if a thought pops into their head, it's likely to come right out of their mouth. While both are outspoken, they will present their thoughts in different manners.

The Peacocks tend to be outgoing in a friendly, jovial, even sarcastic humor sort of way. In fact, we could add "schmoozer" to the Peacock characteristics, as they tend to share their thoughts in a way that makes the recipient always feel complimented.

I realize that the term "schmoozer" may have a negative connotation for some of you. "Brown-noser" may come to mind. Let me clarify here that I truly believe that "schmoozing" (or having the ability to network and make people feel like they are the most important person in the world all the time) is a positive skillset. Yes, I said a positive skillset. But much like any other skillset, there is a time and a place for it. Overdoing anything can make it annoying.

When expressing their thoughts, the Lions are direct. What they think is what you will hear. When the Lions are on task you will rarely find their messages watered down or sugarcoated.

Here's an example of what I mean. If you were late to work, the Peacock might jokingly say something like, "Hey, glad you could join us!" The Lion, on the other hand, might say, "You know you're late, right?" Interestingly, they are both pointing out the same thing to you – that you are late. But the Peacock is most often received better because they schmooze and sugarcoat the message. Don't ever think that your Peacock boss, who just sugarcoated the message, didn't put a note in your employee file about you being late.

The most important thing to learn here is that they are both telling you the same thing. Just because one gives you that message with sprinkles on top doesn't change the message. It changes how you choose to receive the message. Let's read that again…it changes how you CHOOSE to receive the message.

 The final two animals, on the bottom of the chart, are the Lambs and Owls. These two personalities have a low need to direct and are more introverted than their coun-terparts. This doesn't mean they can't lead, it means they prefer not to if given a choice. In addition, introverted does not mean unin-telligent, merely that they are quieter, shy, reserved and/or cautious.

So what does any of this have to do with Myth #2? All four of these personalities have different likes and dislikes, and they have different views on what would be considered rude behavior.

For example, Peacocks and Lambs can become very offended or think it's rude if people don't say good morning, every morning, to every person, or if people aren't nice and friendly. You have to remember that these two personalities are *people or relationship driven*, so of course they are going to be very outgoing, warm and friendly.

On the other hand, Lions and Owls can become very offended or think it's rude to be interrupted, to stand around and chitchat on company time, or to belabor a point. These two personalities are *task driven*. So of course they are going to be very direct, focused, and loyal to time.

So which one is right? Well, that depends on who you ask!

Let me reiterate that every person can exhibit traits from all four of the personality styles. However, we each have one personality that is more predominant than the other three. In an article about DISC insights, "the general population breakdown is that 3% of people are classified as Lions, 11% are Peacocks, 69% are Lambs and 17% are Owls (https://www.discinsights.com/blog/employees/understanding-different-types-of-employees-using-disc).

Based on this article, the majority of people out there are "relationship" driven. It would make sense that they dictate what is considered normal.

As a Lion myself, I have to say that I get very frustrated living in a world where the Peacocks and Lambs dictate what is considered appropriate, rude or normal. If, like me, you are a Lion, or you have a really high Lion as your secondary personality, you have most likely heard statements like these throughout your life:

"You need to learn how to get along with people."

"You need to be nice."

"You need to engage your brain before you open your mouth."

"You need to backpedal."

"Your messages would come across better if you would sugarcoat them a little."

"You need to learn how to socialize so people don't think you're rude."

Lions are consistently being told that they are mean and rude. But here is the question I would like to pose. When was the last time a Peacock or Lamb was told they were rude for being too nice? Here's what I mean.

My ninety-four-year-old mother is a Lamb. As a result, she is very nurturing…not only as a Lamb, but as a Veteran and a mother. She's fabulous at helping me do filing, organize receipts, and get all of my documentation ready for tax prep work. Sometimes, however, she tries too hard to be nice. So much so that it becomes annoying and takes away from my ability to focus on what I'm working on.

One day I was in my office working on a very important project. Mom came in and said she was going to fix lunch and asked if I was hungry. I quickly responded by telling her I was in the middle of a project and I would eat later. Then she said, "Are you sure you're not hungry? It's no bother, I'm fixing lunch anyway." Again I *politely* responded by saying, "No thank you, Mother. I'm not hungry. I'll eat later."

She headed off to the kitchen and started to fix her lunch. She came back in about 15 minutes and asked again if I wanted something to eat while she was fixing lunch. I became a bit frustrated. I had very politely and clearly told her twice that I was not hungry and that I would eat later. By the third time in fifteen minutes of being interrupted, I looked at her and said in a more stern voice, "Mother, I'm not hungry. I will eat later!"

Sure enough, fifteen minutes later, she interrupted me again when she actually brought me lunch. Then she asked if I would like something to drink. I quickly said yes; I didn't have the time or the patience to go through that entire process again!

This is a perfect example of a Lamb personality going out of her way to "be nice" and completely disrespecting my request. Then when I got abrupt with her, she *made the choice* to be offended. Had she respected my first two requests that were delivered respectfully and calmly, she would never have been offended, yet somehow, I am the person being told that I'm rude and that I need to learn how to be nice.

When I share this example, people will often say to me, "Why didn't you just let her bring the lunch and call it a day?" Because this example isn't about my mother bringing me lunch. It's about the lack of respect when I politely gave her the answer…not once, but twice. She doesn't want me to disrespect her, yet she disrespected my polite answer because it wasn't what she wanted to hear. Then she was surprised at the response she received.

Moxie Minute:

People disrespectfully push you to YOUR limits but when you finally set your boundary and fight back, you are the mean one.

This is the very core of how personality differences cause conflict in the workplace or in our personal lives. I have a million of these examples, but I'm sure you get the point. There's an old saying, "Beauty is in the eye of the beholder." It's also important to realize that, "Rude is in the eye of the beholder."

To Peacock and Lamb personalities, being polite is one of <u>the most</u> important characteristics and because of the population statistics I shared earlier, society has adopted this as a norm. We've been taught since childhood, "If you can't say something nice don't say anything at all," and we've read books like *How to Win Friends and Influence People.*

However, if our society focuses on being overly polite and nice to a fault as the ONLY proper response in any situation then we automatically offend two personality types (Lions and Owls). Peacocks and Lambs are automatically nice because of what motivates them, so they don't have to work at this.

But to a Lion and Owl personality, disrespecting their answers or interrupting them while they are working on something important is just as rude as "not being nice" is to a Peacock or a Lamb.

So, while the old myth is "Treat other people the way YOU would like to be treated," it really *should* be "Treat other people the way THEY want to be treated."

Does this new statement hold true in all situations? No.

Here is a rule of thumb to consider. If you are the one who wants or needs something from another person, it is in your best interest to treat other people the way THEY want to be treated as you stand a better chance of connecting with them faster.

For example, if you walk into the office of your Lion boss and you are interrupting your boss then you need to be the one doing the shifting. You can't get your feathers ruffled if that person is abrupt in their response to you. This doesn't mean they don't like you, it means they are busy and don't want to be interrupted.

I experience this phenomenon every time I coach a Peacock or Lamb Rodeo Queen. They literally hire me (a business transaction), via a signed contractual agreement, to provide coaching services for them. My coaching contract is very detailed about my expectations of them as a client. My job as a coach is to get girls out of their comfort zones, teach them new ways of doing things, and prepare them for the roadblocks that they may encounter. Sometimes coaching does not include coddling. Sometimes a girl digs her heels in or refuses to make changes, and when this happens, we may butt heads.

Because they are the ones wanting something, they should be equally responsible for shifting. But alas, they expect me to do 100% of the shifting and if I don't they get their feelings hurt because I'm "rude, mean and a bully." They never stop to think that they were rude to their coach by wasting or abusing my time, taking advantage of my generosities (which is a BIG deal to a Lion), or disrespecting me as a sponsor.

If you ask someone to be your mentor or to coach you (business mentor, pageant coach, etc.), then you have to be willing to work the way they work. You were the one who wanted their help. If they aren't the right mentor or coach for you, simply find another one that suits you better. You don't have to hate people because they are different or because you weren't willing to shift. You just respectfully explain that you are going to go in another direction.

YOUR MOXIE MISSION
(Should You Choose to Accept It)

1. If you haven't ever taken a personality profile, you can start by taking one. The HR department at your company may utilize or recommend one you can take. If that is not an option, there are several online sites where you can take a personality profile. The profile booklet that lines up with the animals I taught in this chapter is the SELF Personality Profile. You can order this booklet at: http://www.nationalseminarstraining.com/Product/Category/Finance/Item/527/index.html, OR go to www.skillpath.com.

2. Once you figure out which personality you are, take time to study the other personalities and how they might be different from you. Examine the things that your personality might do that would be considered rude to another personality.

3. Think about times in the past when someone offended you. Now ask yourself these questions:
   a. Could that person have been a different personality than me and motivated by different things?
   b. Was that person truly trying to offend me, hurt my feelings or insult me, or were they just coming from a different perspective/personality?
   c. Was that person's "motive" to offend me, or did I simply choose to get my feelings hurt because they didn't communicate the way I do?

4. Now make a list of the things you can do to shift your personality when you are working with other people. Where can you make changes, be more understanding, be open to hearing other thoughts, etc.?

CHAPTER 4

I Am Woman, Hear Me Roar

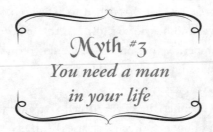

Myth #3
*You need a man
in your life*

My father raised me like the son he never had. Before I could walk, I was riding horses with one of my parents, and it wasn't long thereafter that I was riding on my own. At an early age, I was actively involved in the daily care of the horses and tack (saddles, bridles, and other equipment).

By the time I was in sixth grade, I had already been taught how to drive a truck and trailer and could back that horse trailer into any spot I desired (a skillset that has impressed many a man in my adult years). It started during hay baling season. After the hay fields had been mowed, raked and baled, I would drive the truck and flatbed trailer while my father and others would buck bales of hay onto the flatbed and stack them. This soon led to me hooking up the horse trailers and actually driving on the country gravel roads.

Since I grew up showing horses, I quickly embraced a very competitive spirit. In the equine world, we would go to horse shows throughout the summer (or show season) in order to earn points toward year-end awards. Unfortunately, much to my disappointment, I rarely did well at winning year-end awards. This problem was due to my father working for a company that required him to be "on-call" one weekend per month. This was in the 1970s and we didn't have cell phones, so when Dad was on call with work, he had to stay home close to the phone and be available to leave immediately for work if he was called.

Even though I knew *how* to drive, I wasn't yet licensed to drive so when Dad was on-call, I too had to stay home which meant that I missed yet another horse show and the opportunity to earn points. The competitive person inside me hated on-call weekends because I felt like I was being robbed of my chance to win all-around awards year after year.

I fondly remember the day I turned sixteen and became the proud recipient of my first driver's license. With my infinite sixteen years of wisdom, I quickly deducted that I no longer needed my father to go with me to horse shows, as I could drive myself.

So with great confidence, I sat down with my father and began to plead my case.

"Dad, I've figured out a way to get back in the running for year-end awards," I matter-of-factly stated. "Now that I have my driver's license, I can drive myself to the horse shows."

With a grin on his face, my father replied, "So you want to take my truck, horse trailer, horses and tack, and drive to horse shows by yourself?"

Without batting an eye, I quickly replied, "Yes!"

He responded with, "Well, okay. Here are the truck keys. Take the truck down to the barn, hook up the horse trailer, load everything in you will need at the horse show, load the horses, and meet me down by the pond."

I jumped up, grabbed the keys, gave my dad a hug and ran out the door for the barn. But apparently there was a misunderstanding. You see, when he said, "Okay," I thought he meant, "Yes, you can drive to the horse shows." What I soon figured out was that he meant, "Okay, let's see if you're ready to take on this responsibility."

Thirty minutes later, after hooking up the trailer and loading everything, I drove the "rig" to the pond. There was my dad, sitting in a lawn chair under the big tree next to the pond, drinking a cold beer with a cooler next to him. I stepped out of the truck and watched as my dad began to inspect everything. The trailer hitch was hooked up correctly with the safety chain; the trailer lights were hooked up and functioning properly. The horses were secure in the trailer and the tack (saddles, bridles, blankets and grooming equipment) was accounted for.

What came next is a lesson I will never forget. Dad walked up to me, and cheerfully said, "Great job, girl. Now I would like for you to change all the tires on the rig without unloading the horses."

WHAT? All the tires on the truck and the trailer? That's eight tires! Did I misunderstand him?

I suddenly understood the need for the beer cooler as we were going to be there for a while.

It took me three hours to change those eight tires. I had to jack up the truck four different times and "block" the tires on the trailer four different ways. Breaking the lug nuts was not an easy task and Dad was not offering any assistance. "What do you plan to do if you're out there by yourself and I'm not with you?" he would ask.

At that moment in my life, I just knew my father was trying to prove to me that I couldn't drive to the horse shows by myself. Looking back on this event, however, I realize he was doing quite the opposite. He was proving to himself, and to me, that I *could* handle anything that might happen as I made my way to and from horse shows across the region. My father simply needed to know that since I would have no way of contacting anyone for help, I could get home, or at the very least get to a gas station or pay phone for help.

My list of skills had just been increased to include blocking and changing tires. Independence was mine, and so were those long eluded year-end awards!

As I look back on those first eighteen years, I can quickly acknowledge that my father taught me Moxie! He raised me to be extremely self-sufficient. By observing him year after year, he taught me how to stand up for myself, how to take a stand for what I believed in, and how to have the strength to at least try things before saying I couldn't do it.

I enjoyed spending every moment with my father because it usually meant doing what I enjoyed most: riding horses. As a result I learned how to be a strong, confident woman.

On the flip side of the coin, my mother raised me to be active in the church and involved with music. At a young age I worked in the church teaching Sunday school classes for young kids (go figure – I was a trainer!). As I mentioned earlier, in high school I traveled across the country with a teen gospel group performing at fairs, churches and even in high schools (something you wouldn't see happen today).

While it may not have been her intention, subconsciously she drilled one very strong message into my head growing up, "I just pray that you'll find a mate." A mate? What the hell do you think I am, a gorilla?

I remember being a young woman in my early twenties, on my own, trying to find my way in this big world. I was trying to figure out what my career would be and my mother would continually talk about how she hoped I could find a mate so I would have someone to take care of me and I wouldn't have to be alone.

In all fairness, we have to take into consideration that the message my mother gave me was the one *she* grew up with. You grew up, got married, took care of your husband (in more ways than one) and had children. It was a rite of passage.

In her decade, that message was blatant. Take for example this excerpt from a 1949 Singer Sewing Machine manual. This is the message my mother was trying to live up to. No wonder she was preaching it to me!

Prepare yourself mentally for sewing. Think about what you are going to do...Never approach sewing with a sigh or lackadaisically. Good results are difficult when indifference predominates.

Never try to sew with a sink full of dirty dishes or beds unmade. When there are urgent housekeeping chores, do these first so your mind is free to enjoy your sewing. When you sew, make yourself as attractive as possible. Put on a clean dress. Keep a little bag full of French chalk near your sewing machine to dust your fingers at intervals. Have your hair in order, powder and lipstick put on. If you are constantly fearful that a visitor will drop in or your husband will come home, and you will not look neatly put together, you will not enjoy your sewing.

Uh...wow! That's all I can say. First of all, do you notice the assumption is that you HAVE a husband who will come home and find you not "put together"? Mom, I'm so sorry you had to live up to those expectations!

But times were changing and women had options. Nevertheless, I heard that message often and subconsciously, I suppose, acted on it. Finally, at the age of twenty-seven, I met, dated, and married the perfect man...for my mother!

First, and most important to my mother, we met in church. He was attending a Christian college, and carrying a double bachelor's in computer science and mathematics (which he completed in three years). He loved sports. Not horses or rodeo...but softball. So I started playing on co-ed softball leagues so we would share activities. That lasted until I tore up my knee.

Two months after we were married, my father passed away and one month after that, my new husband lost his college job. Unfortunately, the honeymoon was over before it even got started.

He ended up securing a great job with a major telecommunications company that offered great benefits. About a year later, I started taking night classes at the junior college to try to work toward my degree. So, now I was married, working full-time, not pursuing any of the things I loved and trying to get a college degree at night. Look out American dream, here I come!

Yep, it was perfect. Just not perfect for me. Unfortunately, after three years the marriage was over and my college career was put on hold temporarily. I had to re-arrange my life and get my feet firmly planted before moving forward with anything.

My ex-husband married again as soon after our divorce as the law would allow. As fate would have it, his second wife had the same first *and* middle name as me. Not realizing this was happening, I had made the decision to keep my married name of Fox so I wouldn't have to go through the long drawn-out procedure of changing my name on all legal documents. Besides that, Fox just seemed like a much better name than Brown!

So, now there were two women with the exact same name, with marriages to the same man. It wasn't long before our financial records began to bleed together and I was soon being stopped in retail establishments and gas stations for having written bad checks. Just for the record, the bad checks were not mine. Amazing how hard it is to prove that when your social security number is on the check…hmm.

My attorney clearly told me that I did not have enough money to fight this battle and he suggested that the best course of action would be to leave town and start over somewhere else.

Without hesitation, I packed up and moved to Kirksville, Missouri, where I had old rodeo friends who were attending college. I finally secured a job at Northeast Missouri State University (today known as Truman State University) as the administrative assistant to the assistant academic dean. Since I had to work full-time and part-time to support myself and I was now in my early thirties, going back to college was not as easy as one might think. I talk about this more in chapter nine, "College and Knowledge Are Not the Same Thing".

I had officially started my life over – the first of several start-overs that I would experience in my lifetime.

Does anyone see a challenge with these mixed messages? My father raised me to be completely self-sufficient, and my mother raised me to be dependent on a man.

Now I realize that today you can have both. I acknowledge that by today's standards you can be a strong woman and find a partner who loves you and compliments you. You can have a career and children. You can be successful at home and at work.

Unfortunately, that wasn't the message I received. I was led to believe that a man needed to "take care of me" and I should take care of his needs because that was my "duty." Anyone who knows me knows that message did not sit well with me, even though I tried desperately to take that route.

The point I'm trying to make is in today's world a woman can have it all if that is her choice. But a woman doesn't NEED a partner in her life to be complete. Believing that they are incomplete without a partner sets so many women up for disappointment, broken hearts, and wasted years invested with the wrong people.

Many women reading this may have been brought up with the same mixed message as I was about needing a man to be complete. As I look back over my life, I realize that every man I dated, I would take on *their* hobbies, and *their* likes and dislikes in the hopes that they would like me and want to be with me. Instead, I should have been looking for a partner who had common interests and who would take an interest in me and my hobbies and likes and dislikes.

That all began to change after my divorce was final. I didn't have a real desire to get involved in another long-term relationship. However, I did date a bit here and there.

I dated one man in particular whom I met while having some work done on my car. We would go to dinner, go dancing, we enjoyed music, went to the lake with groups, watched ball games on TV and enjoyed each other's company.

On my thirtieth birthday, my crazy group of friends decided that we needed to have a toga pool party to celebrate my birthday. Since they were handing out invitation fliers to everyone they met, the guest list grew rapidly.

Of course, I had invited the man I was dating to the party and was excited to be surrounded by my friends and my date on my birthday.

The party day arrived. I received a call around noon from my date informing me that he would not be able to come to the party. He didn't provide any explanation, so I asked him if he had to work. He responded with a simple, "No." Sensing a strange vibe over the phone, I pushed for an explanation.

"Debra, I'm not going to be able to attend the party, and I think we need to stop seeing each other," he said.

His comment caught me off guard. After all, it was my birthday and you just don't expect someone to break up with you on your birthday. So I asked him, "Has something happened that I'm unaware of?"

"No."

"Well, then, what seems to be the problem?"

He responded with, "This just isn't something that I wanted to talk about over the phone. I'm really not comfortable having this conversation with you right now."

Now my curiosity was just too much to bear. There had to be something that caused this sudden change in his attitude toward me.

So I quickly replied, "Well given the fact that we aren't going to be seeing each other anymore, over the phone is the only option you have and inquiring minds want to know what the heck is going on. Since it's my birthday, that's the least you owe me."

His answer was not what I expected. "Well...my friends are giving me crap about dating a woman who weighs more than I do and even though I've had more fun going out with you than anyone I've ever dated, I just can't deal with my friends giving me crap!"

The cat was out of the bag. Clearly this was not the answer I was expecting. It was about here that my Moxie kicked in. Within seconds of him sharing his reasoning, I started to laugh. I laughed for several minutes and said, "That's the funniest thing I've ever heard."

As you can imagine, his answer was, "Well, this isn't the response I expected."

"Well, what did you expect?"

"I was afraid I would hurt your feelings and that was the last thing I wanted to do."

Before I could catch myself, the reply came flying out of my mouth. "Hurt my feelings? Why would that hurt my feelings? I'm not used to dating a man with a pee wee as small as yours, but I didn't realize that body parts were a deciding factor in dating you. Had I known that, I would have ended this relationship sooner. At least I can lose weight. What do you plan to do to fix your problem?"

His response was priceless. "That wasn't very nice!"

REALLY?!

After the bomb he had dropped on me, I wasn't too concerned about being nice, but to have him verbalize it was even funnier to me and I continued to laugh. I caught my breath, gained my composure and said, "Thank you for sharing your concerns. I have a party to get ready for, so it's time for me to get off the phone."

I have to be honest and tell you that I did allow this to put a little bit of a damper on my birthday party that evening, and I most likely had a bit of a pity party for myself.

Three days later, however, he called back, apologizing for what he had done. He wanted to get back together and said he had made a huge mistake.

"Yes, you did!" I quickly responded. "Your apology is accepted, but I am no longer interested in seeing you."

I'm sure most of you reading this are saying, "Way to set him straight, Debra! But people make mistakes. At least he apologized and was admitting that he made the mistake. Didn't he deserve another chance?"

Yes, people make mistakes, but let's not forget, he wasn't planning on talking with me about his concerns or fears. He was just going to break up with me, without any explanation, ON MY BIRTHDAY, three hours before my party! And he made it clear that what his friends thought was more important than following his own path. I simply did not feel that was the behavior of someone who really cared about me, or who I needed in my life.

We all know that men want what they seemingly can't have. I truly believed he called and wanted to get back together because I had dismissed him without showing any hurt feelings of losing him, so his apology had no depth in my book.

How many women would have accepted his apology and taken him back? How many women would have lowered their own expectations, lowered their own self-worth and accepted someone back who had treated them in that manner?

Over the years I've watched as countless friends focused all of their energies on finding a man so they wouldn't be alone, and I watched as many of them, just like I had done, invested months with toxic partners all in the name of having someone in their life. I watched as they repeated that cycle over and over and over…usually with the same results.

Moxie Minute:

Losing someone you care about hurts!
But losing someone who doesn't respect and
appreciate you
is actually a gain, not a loss!

When I turned thirty-five, and was sick and tired of the cycle, I had a Moxie meeting with myself. I can remember it like it was yesterday. I was standing in the bathroom, brushing my teeth when this powerful emotion came over me. I looked at myself in the mirror, and out loud I said to myself, "You may end up spending the rest of your life alone and you need to be okay with that *right now!*"

That was the most liberating moment of my life. To accept that I no longer needed a man in my life meant that I no longer needed to constantly be looking for one, and that was the day I stopped looking. That was the day my true life began.

Not only did I have to set a boundary with myself, I had to set a really hard boundary with the one person who had been giving me this message for three decades – my mother. I explained to her that I no longer wanted to hear from her how I needed a man to make me complete, or to take care of me, or to pay the bills. I asked her to accept the fact that I could take care of myself and I told her this was non-negotiable. Surprisingly, she heard me loud and clear, respected my request and it has never been mentioned again.

Now, don't take me wrong. If the *right* man came along, I would be delighted to have a healthy relationship, but I was done with the unhealthy, draining, toxic men who I had *allowed* into my life because I was looking for a mate. The desperation to please my mother and find someone to take care of me had taken over my self-worth, sound judgment and eventually my happiness.

Some of you have been fortunate enough to find your soul mate, the person in your life who completes you. Congratulations! Build your relationship, your life together, and your family. In the process, don't lose sight of YOU. Don't forget to take care of you.

My experience is that there are women who are either married or single, who are struggling with how to survive, how to achieve success and how to be happy. Somewhere along the line, you either put your happiness in the hands of someone else, or you believe that because you didn't find your soul mate that there is something wrong with you and you are stuck in the muck and mire.

If you can relate to these feelings, it's time for some Moxie motivation!

No matter your situation the single most important rule is one that I hear every single time I board an airplane:

"Please put the oxygen mask on yourself before attempting to assist those around you."

Even today, women are still taught the underlying message that we need to take care of everyone else first. Our family, our bosses, our company, our volunteer duties, our church family…and the list goes on. At some point, with this grueling schedule, you will burn out. The reality is if your vessel is empty, you have nothing to give to others. If you are suffering from burnout or depression, your perspective on life will be altered.

Therefore, it is imperative that you put the oxygen mask on yourself first. Figure out what floats your boat, flips your switch, peels your banana, and fills your vessel. What makes your heart sing? What makes you happy and brings joy into your life?

Only you can figure out what this is for you. It might be gardening, painting, singing, or exercise. Maybe you love spending time with your grandchildren, or volunteering for charitable organizations.

Whatever it is, schedule time for it. Not once or twice a year but regularly. This needs to be a priority for you so you are continually filling your vessel. Then and only then will you have the energy, power, motivation and Moxie to be successful at your life and to give to the other people who matter to you the most.

In the next chapters we'll talk more about the things we need to do to protect ourselves, promote ourselves, and find our inner Moxie.

Moxie Minute:

When you start seeing your worth,
you'll find it's harder to stay around people who don't!

YOUR MOXIE MISSION
(Should You Choose to Accept It)

1. If you are married to your soul mate, make sure you are still putting the oxygen mask on yourself so you don't burn out. Jump to #4.

2. If you are married and struggling in your marriage, please seek out professional assistance in learning how to rebuild, refuel, or re-engage in the relationship. In the meantime, a good place to start is by putting the oxygen mask on you first. Jump to #4.

3. If you are single and struggling with not having someone in your life, it may be time for you to be more detailed about what you are looking for and what you offer to a relationship.

   a. Are you secure and happy living life alone? Are you achieving your successes alone?

   b. If not, you most likely won't be happy or achieve success with someone else either.

   c. When you are desperately looking for a partner, you will settle!

   d. You may have to have a Moxie moment with yourself in front of the mirror like I did. Acknowledge to yourself, out loud, that you MAY be alone for quite some time and you need to be okay with that right now. Then, get up and live your life for you. Be happy, be secure, be successful and you stand a much better chance of attracting not only the right potential partner, but the right people in general into your life.

4. The very first thing you need to do is sit down and start making a list of the things that make *your* heart sing. What brings you joy, makes you smile or laugh?
5. For the purpose of this exercise, your list should <u>not</u> include taking care of someone else. This exercise is all about YOU!
6. Once you complete your list, pick one or two of the things you listed and schedule time to do them <u>this week</u>. Make it the priority, not the "if I have time left over I'll see if I can squeeze that in." Remember, your "vehicle" needs fuel to keep going. You always stop at the gas station first!
    a. Don't start making excuses. Figure out how to make it happen.
    b. Example: if you have "get a pedicure" on your list (I know I do!), but you have budget concerns, search in your area for a cosmetology school. These young people are in training, need people to work on and the prices are very reasonable.
7. After the first week, schedule time in your calendar every single week for YOU! Put the oxygen mask on YOU. Do something on your list every week for YOU!

CHAPTER 5

The Road to Success is an Eight-Lane Highway Under Construction

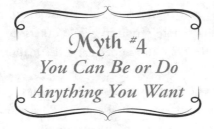

Myth #4
You Can Be or Do Anything You Want

Because I work from home, there are days when I just need a break from the computer or the phone and in order to get away from my work, I have to get up and leave the house. Many times I don't have a specific destination in mind when I get in the car, only that I just want to go somewhere. I start the car, pull out of the driveway and then drive around hoping that a destination will pop into my head. Usually, however, I end up driving around in circles for thirty to forty-five minutes and then go right back home. Can you relate? Businesses, corporations and organizations can often deal with the same issue.

Many years ago, in order to get a large ship out of port, several small tug boats would be attached to all corners and sides of the ship. Can you imagine what would happen if those tug boats were all pulling in different directions, or if they were completely unaware of the destination they were trying to reach? In order to be successful at getting a ship out of port, the tug boats had to work together, pulling in the same direction and moving toward the same destination.

This is the reason why every successful company or organization creates and follows a mission statement. By doing so, they stand a much better chance of having all team members working together toward the same destination.

So why would this practice be any less important in your personal life?

Each person has the luxury and responsibility of determining what their personal and/or career destination will be. Some take this responsibility more seriously, while others just get up every day, head out the door and hope that a destination will pop into their head.

Reaching a destination requires three things:

1. Determine your destination(s)
2. Map your route to reach your destination (program your life GPS)
3. Take action — Create habits that will support your journey

DETERMINE YOUR DESTINATION

First, we have to determine what our possible destinations are — our goals. This brings me to another myth or half-truth, a statement I hear quite often, that can literally delay or derail selecting the correct destination:

"You can be or do anything you want!"

I can see why this statement might be considered motivational. The intent is to encourage people to reach for the stars and go for the gold. Parents say it to their children to encourage them to strive for success. Bosses say it to team members to encourage them to learn different crafts in the industry. "You can do anything you want, if you just set your mind to it."

I agree that an individual can and *should* set and pursue goals. I also agree that we should have destinations and work to reach those destinations. But as I discussed in chapter two "What Is Success?" I believe that each person has a unique destination or definition of success.

I regularly teach about the importance of setting goals (selecting destinations) in your life.

Research and statistics have confirmed that by writing your goals down, you stand a seventy percent greater chance of achieving those goals. This is the reason why so much emphasis is placed on not only setting your goals but also writing them down. Companies implement this same strategy by having managers go over the goals for next year with each employee during employee performance reviews. The goals are in writing and agreed upon so everyone knows what the expectation is.

Much like the gentleman in my seminar, people will tell me they don't believe that writing goals down really makes a difference. I believe this is because we don't understand why it works.

In our brain there is this thing called the Reticular Activating System (RAS). For lack of a better explanation, this is your brain's radar. Most of you have experienced this at some point in your life. Here's my personal favorite example. Think back to the last time you bought a car, new or used. Some of you researched for weeks *before* you bought the car while some of you walked on the lot, picked out a car and bought it. Either way, there may have been a point where you started seeing your car everywhere you went. And not just your car, you may have actually seen your model and color.

What do you think is more feasible? That people went out, bought your car and were stalking you OR that your brain was more tuned in to what you had researched, thought about, driven and had on your mind more lately? Your brain was more tuned in!

This is what happens when you write your goals down or make vision boards (see end of chapter for the definition of a vision or dream board). It puts your dream in front of you daily, reminding your brain what it is you are supposed to be working and focusing on. This is setting your life GPS on the course you have selected.

When I look back over my childhood, I don't recall my parents ever telling me, "You can be or do anything you want to be or do." It was simply not a discussion we ever had. In spite of that, I grew up having dreams of setting and achieving big goals. I was a big dreamer with an entrepreneurial spirit.

I officially became an entrepreneur in second grade. Our school didn't have air conditioning systems, so in the spring and fall the teachers would open the windows in the classrooms to let in fresh air. Of course, bugs and flies would come into the room as well, and after a few days they would die. We would end up with dead flies and bugs all over the classroom and I began to notice that the little boys in my class were playing with the dead bugs.

During one of our arts and craft times, we were making things with basal wood (the lightweight wood used to make model airplanes). This was back in the day when they still gave X-Acto knives to second graders! While all the other little girls in the class were making doll furniture, I was making fly coffins. Yes, you heard me right. Fly coffins. I would cut out lids and then paint them in different motifs. I then became an event planner by orchestrating fly burials in the sandbox during recess. Since I was the only person making fly coffins, I had the corner on the market. I sold the fly coffins for a penny each. Talk about great profit margins. I was making a 100% profit because I had no overhead... the school was providing all my materials.

This was how I got bubble gum and candy money!

From a very young age, I just had this natural ability to be a strategic thinker, to think outside the box, and to figure out how to do whatever I wanted to do, even though I had never been given that message growing up. In fact, due to financial restrictions and other concerns, my parents would often discourage me from "pursuing my lofty dreams." But I had goals! My challenge was that often my goals were not realistic based on my skillsets.

If you believe that you can go through life without setting goals or determining your destinations, that is the biggest myth of them all! While bosses, friends and family may offer tons of advice on what, when, where, how and why you "should" do something, ultimately <u>you</u> are the only person who can program your life GPS to determine your destinations (goals) in life. Which one you choose and how you choose to live your life is completely up to you. Your job is to research, get advice, process the information and then determine the best course of action for you based on your definition of success, your personal skillsets, and your passions.

In more recent years, however, I continuously hear people tell their children, siblings, or subordinates, "You can be or do anything you want" in an effort to motivate and encourage them to achieve great things. "Set your goals high and soar!"

My observation is that it never really mattered what these children or people were trying to do, they were told they could do it without any strategic or realistic thought given to the goal at hand.

This phenomenon really made an impact on me when *American Idol* hit the airwaves. Because I had owned a modeling and talent agency, I was very intrigued with the show's concept. I love shows that encourage people to pursue their dreams rather than reality shows that highlight trauma and drama. So, I tuned in weekly to watch as literally thousands of people would line up for a chance to audition in front of the panel of celebrity judges.

I truly believed because it was a nationally televised show, that the auditions would be fabulous. I can remember sitting in front of the TV, waiting with baited breath to hear great performances and see feel-good stories. Instead, I often found myself screaming at the TV, "Who in the hell told you that you could sing?"

I'll tell you who. The same people that kept telling these poor schmucks, "You can be or do anything you set your mind to. If you want to be a singer, then you go to those auditions." These well-meaning people were either making fun of these hopefuls, didn't want to hurt their feelings so they encouraged them in spite of their true opinions, or they simply did not know any better.

Week after week I would just shake my head and think back to when I owned my modeling and talent agency. During that time, I regularly interviewed men and women of all ages who had dreams and goals of becoming a model, actor or performer. They would make an appointment to come to my office to meet with a model/talent agent hoping that we could make all their dreams come true. Over the years, I looked through hundreds of portfolios and listened to even more vocal and acting auditions.

I would ask these young ingénues, "Why did you come in to see me today?" Let me assure you, I heard every answer under the sun.

"Every time our daughter gets her school photos done, the photographer tells us that our daughter is beautiful and should be a model."

"I had a modeling portfolio created by our local small town photographer and he said I have a huge modeling career ahead of me."

"I've competed in several singing competitions and I want to pursue a singing career."

"Have you ever won or placed in a competition?" I would ask.

"No, but everyone told me I should come back."

Well what did you expect them to tell you? "You suck! Please don't pay us any more money to enter our pageant, competition, or to get a photo shoot again."?

I've learned over the years that when people give you "advice" regarding your dreams and goals, it is imperative that you take a step back and see how much they stand to benefit from what they are telling you.

Why in the world would anyone tell you that you are pursuing the wrong career or goal if it meant you wouldn't come back to their company or organization and spend money?

Don't misunderstand my point. I do believe that people have the right to be paid for their services. I'm not suggesting that you shouldn't have to pay for help and guidance. As a pageant coach, I charge a small fee to coach girls who are competing in pageants, but it is not my livelihood. I do this primarily to make it a business relationship, to see how committed they are and to put a price on their dedication. But we all know those people who will tell you whatever you want to hear so you'll come back and invest more, spend more and share more about their organization.

On *American Idol*, I always found it amazing how everyone thought Simon Cowell (one of the original judges) was so mean, rude, and crass in giving feedback to the contestants. More times than not, I found his feedback accurate, honest and timely. Simon Cowell could give honest feedback because he didn't make money directly from the contestants if they made it onto the show. So when you think about it, his feedback was the most genuine and he was doing so many of those contestants a huge favor by steering them in the right direction.

Here's the point I'm trying to make. I personally believe the statement, "You can be or do anything you want" is a half-truth. While it is intended to motivate people, unfortunately it is one of the most misleading statements ever uttered. The huge misconception that comes with this statement is the part that is usually missing. The statement should be:

"You can be or do anything you want, AS LONG AS you have the skillset and the willingness to do whatever it takes to achieve it."

There are two key concerns with this half-truth.

First, and most obviously, telling someone that they can be or do anything they want without defining any parameters could be extremely misleading or create false hope. More importantly, it could cause people to focus tremendous amounts of time and effort toward the wrong destination. How many hours might someone waste chasing the wrong goal for the wrong reason, simply because well-meaning family and friends told them, "You did great," when in reality they barely did mediocre? And even IF someone is able to achieve success within an industry, if it isn't the right career they might spend their life being miserable. Successful, but miserable.

I remember one particular young lady in my agency. She was a very special personality and worked very hard to learn and perfect the modeling and acting skills we taught. One day she came to me and said she was competing for a state pageant in the Miss America system and needed to decide which talent she was going to perform. I asked her what she was considering and her immediate answer was, "A vocal performance." When I asked her why she had selected a vocal performance, I expected her to tell me that she loved singing, that it was her passion, and that she couldn't imagine doing anything else in the competition. Instead, she said, "The pageant organizers and coaches told me that if I want to win the pageant, I have to do a vocal performance because vocal performances always win." Well alrighty then!

So, I asked her to sing a song for me. After she sang her song, she looked at me and said, "What do you think?" Apparently my disapproval was all over my face and she said, "What's wrong?"

"Nothing's wrong, but what else do you have?"

She looked at me with shock and asked, "You didn't like that?"

"I liked it fine. My question is, do you want to win?"

Hesitantly she replied, "I'm afraid if I don't do what they told me to do that I won't stand a chance."

"You don't stand a chance if you sing either," I quickly responded.

Now before you start thinking that I'm just a cruel person who didn't take her feelings into account, let's back up and review. She came to me asking what she should do for the talent portion of the pageant. As her agent, I considered it my job to give her honest feedback instead of status quo feedback. I was not successful as an agent unless my models and talent were successful and based on what I had heard, she was not going to experience success by singing in that pageant. (Later in this book, when I talk about the "Parable of the Bird", I want you to think back to this story.)

Again I asked her, "What else do you have?" She sheepishly smiled at me and shared that she had prepared a monologue. "Let me hear it," I said.

Without batting an eye, she passionately delivered a monologue from the movie *Steel Magnolias*. She had selected the graveyard scene where Sally Fields has the emotional meltdown after burying her daughter. She flawlessly delivered the scene and by the time she was done I had tears running down my face. I sat there in silence. She stepped out of character, gathered herself, looked at me and said, "What do you think about that as an option?"

What did I think? "UNBELIEVABLE!" was all I could say! I told her that if she didn't deliver that monologue at the pageant she was crazy, regardless what anyone else had told her.

I can't even begin to tell you how elated I was to know that she took my advice. She went to that pageant, delivered the monologue, and while she did not win the pageant, she did win the talent award even though she didn't sing a song.

Within the next year, I took her with a group of models and actors from my agency to an international model and talent convention, where she repeated the monologue performance in an acting category. Not only did she win the Overall Acting Award (from all acting age divisions), she won the Overall Talent Award (from all age divisions in all performance categories).

This is a great example of a young woman who could NOT, in fact, do anything she wanted to do. She "wanted" to sing in that pageant because everyone told her that is what she needed to do to win. But clearly that was not where her true talents were. She was an okay singer, but singing would not have allowed her to shine at her maximum potential.

Back in the eighties, after representing Kansas in the Miss Rodeo America Pageant, I teamed up with another former Miss Rodeo Kansas to create The Competitive Edge. We provided coaching services and Rodeo Queen clinics for young women competing in the Rodeo Queen world. Within two short years, we were honored to assist four young women to fulfill their dreams of winning a national title.

Much like any kind of career or life coach, one of the most difficult parts of being a pageant coach is being willing to deliver the messages that the girls aren't hearing from anyone else. I could give countless examples of young women who have been told by their family and friends that they can do anything they want without being given any real, candid, honest feedback about what that is going to take.

Every single year, young women win state titles and then prepare to compete for Miss Rodeo America. Throughout the year, every person they come in contact with tells them, "You've got this, girl," "You're going to rock the Miss Rodeo America Pageant," "You have everything it takes to win this!"

Then I come along and have to dispel those well-meaning but very misleading myths. I have to say things like, "You don't have this! There is much more work that has to be done!" Suddenly, I'm the evil bitch who is bullying kids. I become the Simon Cowell of the Rodeo Queen world.

Unfortunately, young women will compete over and over, never being told what the challenge is or what is holding them back. When the pageant is over, I watch as pageant directors walk up to them and say, "Please tell me you're going to come back next year. You were awesome!"

There are times when the contestants don't see any scores from the pageants, they aren't given feedback from the judges and no one really holds them accountable for the things they need to do to be competitive. So these young women are spinning their wheels and spending money trying to be or do anything they want but not focusing on the required skillsets necessary to win, or committing to do whatever it takes to win.

John Maxwell, one of my favorite corporate authors and speakers, talks about this very issue and wrote about it on his blog at http://www.johnmaxwell.com/blog/do-you-have-what-it-takes.

Does your dream align with your natural abilities?

Olympic sprinters spend countless hours learning how to accelerate out of the starting blocks and to perfect their stride. With years of practice, they're able to shave precious fractions of a second off of the time it takes them to complete a race. However, in actuality, every world-class sprinter began his or her athletic career with loads of inborn ability. Absent of God-given talent, the average person, even after years of disciplined training, could not hope to keep pace with these elite runners.

In my experience, a person can only improve about one or two notches above their natural talent in a given area. For example, if on a scale of 1-10 you happen to be a "3" as a singer, then taking voice lessons and music appreciation courses may lift you to a "4." If you're especially diligent in studying how to sing, you may even improve to a "5." Even so, you've only improved from bad to average—and people don't pay to hear an average singer. The formula for success is to build your career around skills in which you're already a "7" or an "8" and to spend your time perfecting them.

Clearly, you can TRY to be or do anything you want. Unfortunately, if your natural gifts/skills aren't complimentary to your goal, you may not experience the level of success you hope for. As John Maxwell says, the success formula is to focus your destination choices around your natural seven or eight skills and spend time perfecting them. You must first make sure that your destinations (goals, dreams) align with your natural abilities.

I can completely relate to what John Maxwell is saying. While I traveled with a semi-professional singing group in high school, and have been blessed with a singing talent, I can without a doubt tell you that I was not cut out to be a professional vocal entertainer. Why? I have a major flaw. I simply cannot remember the words to a song. When I get on stage to sing alone, I have a complete memory lapse and then have a panic attack.

But here is the interesting part. I can stand on a stage in front of hundreds of people as a speaker and have no fear whatsoever. I can speak from my heart and I share things on the platform that I can't even remember when I'm done. It's like I become another person.

So while I could sing, and traveled and performed with bands for many years, I could not become a professional solo artist. However, as a result of those opportunities, I gained massive experience about vocal performance, stage and microphone usage, sound equipment and band promotions. I combined that experience with my natural entrepreneurial drive when I opened my modeling and talent agency. I was able to figure out what my seven and eight skills were and made the transition.

This is exactly what you want to do as you go through life. Take advantage of experiences...all of them. Learn from those experiences and then put those new skills and knowledge in your bag of tricks. But, invest the majority of your time focusing on and improving your seven and eight skills along the way. Don't get distracted.

MAP YOUR TRIP

Once you have your goals determined, and in writing, your next step is to plan the course of action necessary to achieve that goal or reach that destination. This is what I call "setting your life GPS".

Let me explain what I mean. If you decide your destination goal is to drive from New York City to Los Angeles, but you just hop in the car without a map or a GPS system, would you reach your destination? Most people will agree that "eventually" is the most appropriate answer. Is there a more direct route? Yes!

Obviously, if you are planning a long trip, you will reach your destination more quickly if you plan a route and closely follow your plan. Reaching your personal destinations (goals) is the exact same way.

Let's say your destination/goal is to get promoted in your company within the next twelve months. Great goal! But now you have to figure out what it is going to take to get you from where you are to where you want to be. Here are the things you might want to consider:

- What type of positions or departments are you interested in?
- What are the requirements needed to advance to that position or department?
- Do you have the skills, education, experience, etc.?
- If yes, who do you need to talk to about your career goal? Your boss, the manager of the department you want to move into? It's important that you put your desires out there, instead of sitting around and waiting on someone to "discover" you. Let people know you are interested and ask them for advice or suggestions.
- If no, would it benefit you to have a mentor within your company to guide you?
- Would it benefit you to talk to your boss about attending seminars for additional training?
- Do you need to simply invest in your own additional education if the company won't pay for it? If so, where can you take night classes or online classes to achieve that?

This is just an example. The point I'm making is that in order to map out the route necessary to reach your destination/goal, you need to do your own due diligence (research) and find out what you need to do.

HABITS

You've picked your destinations, and you've invested time researching, studying and preparing for your trip. You have the information necessary to program your life GPS. Now what?

DO IT! Take action. Get in your life vehicle, start the engine and start moving! Don't wait for the perfect time, or the perfect opportunity, or the perfect partner, or the perfect sponsor. Just go DO IT! Start your journey toward your destination.

Now, we all know that no matter how prepared and planned you are, life will throw things at you. You *will* experience detours, roadblocks and unexpected stops along the way. You'll be driving along, working hard and all of a sudden you find yourself on an eight-lane interstate surrounded by crazy drivers, detours, and roadblocks. This is the point where so many people take the next exit, park their life and say, "Life got in the way!"

This is where Moxie comes in. Having the determination, fortitude and guts to keep moving toward your goal no matter what life throws at you. Just know that as long as you are clear about a destination, you can always recalculate your life GPS to a new route any time and keep going.

I can remember when I competed for Miss Rodeo Kansas the second time. The first time I competed, I was a hot mess and could only call it a learning experience. But after losing, I spent the next year incorporating what I had learned, studying, riding every day and putting together a wardrobe the best I could with the very limited budget I had. You know when people talk about having a shoestring budget? Do you know those little plastic tips on the end of a shoestring? THAT was my budget!

A week before the pageant, I received a call from my mother who proceeded to announce to me that if I won the pageant, I would have to turn it down because she and my father were "not going to pay for me to gallivant all over the country."

Now before everyone gets up in arms about how my parents didn't support me, let me clarify. My parents had just spent a tremendous amount of money building their retirement home and moving from Illinois to Kansas to retire. In hindsight, I'm sure my mother was catching hell from my father and they were concerned that they would not be *able* to financially support me. But unfortunately that is not how the message came across.

What I heard, and quite honestly what was said, was that they *wouldn't* pay for me to gallivant. I was infuriated to say the least.

I believe that this spurred on my very first Moxie moment. I kept thinking to myself, "Why even bother going if I'm expected to turn it down IF I'm fortunate enough to win?" Then it hit me. "I'm not going to turn it down and that is the end of that!"

As I drove my car and trailer into the empty rodeo grounds in Strong City, Kansas, I found my mom and dad, who had arrived early to set up a camping spot for the weekend. We were the only people on the grounds. I pulled up to the truck and camper, opened my car door, stepped out and proclaimed, "I'd like to call a family round-table discussion."

In our family when there was an issue, I was always called to a round-table discussion. But *this* was the first round-table discussion that I had called and I'm sure it caught my mom and dad completely off guard.

I was shaking in my boots (literally), but I mustered up enough courage to firmly but respectfully say, "Dad, are you aware that Mom called me this past week and told me that if I win this, I have to turn it down?" They just looked at each other. "Well here is my response," I continued. "I don't recall asking you to pay for me to gallivant. I'm working a full-time job as a finance manager and a part-time job at Shepler's Western Store to pay for the things I need. I'm here to win this year and if you aren't on board with that, then I would suggest you pack up and go home because I don't need any negative vibes here while I'm competing."

BAM — my first Moxie moment was in the books. And there was no more talk about turning down any awards. I ended up winning Miss Rodeo Kansas that year and went on to compete at Miss Rodeo America. While I truly was not prepared for that title, I again walked away with tons of experience that has helped me reach my destinations in life.

I've had to rely on Moxie to get me through everything in my life, including getting jobs. I'll talk more about that, in chapter six, "When Life Hands You Lemons".

Moxie Minute:

*"If you can't figure out your purpose, figure out your passion.
For your passion will lead you right into your purpose."*
Bishop T.D. Jakes

YOUR MOXIE MISSION
(Should You Choose To Accept It)

In order to "be or do anything you want to be or do," you will want to take these steps:

1. Do self-discovery. Know YOU! What are your likes and dislikes? What are your natural abilities, strengths and skillsets? With training, education or practice can you improve those skills?

2. No matter how old you are or where you are in your life, you can create a list of possible "destinations." Figure out what it is you want to achieve, personally and/or professionally.
   a. School activities
   b. Pageant participation
   c. College major
   d. Career
   e. Advancement in your career
   f. Starting your own business
   g. Finding the right partner
   h. Starting a charitable organization

3. Be VERY detailed in outlining what the destination looks like. If you succeed at reaching the destination, how will you know?

4. Research what skills or requirements will be necessary to reach your destinations

5. Review your current skillsets and strengths to determine if there is a gap between your current strengths and what is required. This step requires a hardcore honest look at you. This is not about finding fault, it's about finding gaps

that need to be filled between point A and point B in your journey to your destination.

6. Determine what it will take to improve your skills and reduce the gap.
   a. More dedicated practice
   b. More education (schooling, seminars, specialty clinics, etc.)
   c. IF the destination you are seeking has specific physical appearance criteria, you may need to be willing to change your physical appearance (lose weight, bulk up, change hairstyle, learn how to apply make-up, change wardrobe, etc.) — we'll talk more about this in a later chapter
   d. Improve your speaking skills (join Toastmasters, take speech classes, attend seminars on how to speak)
   e. Make appropriate contacts
7. OR find out if the gap is too large to focus that much time and energy trying to improve. Maybe there are other natural abilities where you need to be investing your time.
8. Make a vision (dream) board. A vision board is typically a poster board or surface (bathroom mirror, back of your bedroom door, etc.) where you create a collage using pictures you've torn out of magazines that represent your goals, dreams and visions. When you surround yourself with images of who you want to become, what you want to have, where you want to live, or where you want to vacation, your RAS begins to focus and you begin to take different actions which in turn allows your life to change to match those desires.

CHAPTER 6

Here's Your Lemon!

Myth #5
*When Life Hands You
Lemons...
Make Lemonade*

L et me start by sharing with you that this is the second time I've written this chapter. God truly has a sense of humor!

Anyone who is familiar with the Blue Collar Comedy Network knows Bill Engvall, who is a comedian in that group. He has become quite famous for his classic "here's your sign" comedy routine.

Have you ever had one of those days when you know that life is looking at you and saying, "Here's your lemon"? Like you don't have anything else to do except put out another fire or deal with another trauma.

You know the advice that has been handed down through the decades. "When life hands you lemons, make lemonade." This myth is the optimists' anthem. We've all heard it, and we all know exactly what it means. When in life you are dealing with difficult lessons, disappointments, hard times, losses or very sour situations, you just need to figure out how to turn those negatives into a positive.

Sounds good in theory, right? In reality though, I don't believe it's quite that simple.

Several years ago, I read another quote about lemons and lemonade:

"Unless life also gives you water and sugar, your lemonade is going to suck!"

If life hands you lemons, you can certainly squeeze those lemons to death, collect the juice in a pitcher and drink it. The truth of the matter is, without sugar and water your lemonade is going to be very sour and very difficult to swallow.

I don't know about anyone else in the world, but my experiences have taught me that rarely does life hand me lemons and then hand me a second course of sugar and water. I've learned over the years that I usually have to go looking for or provide the sugar and water myself.

Too many times, people get stuck holding the lemons, staring at the lemons, talking about the lemons, and even squeezing the lemons. Unfortunately, they miss the most important step!

In order to survive life's dramas and traumas, you must be willing to look for (or create) the *sweetness* in the situation (sugar), and you may need to *dilute* (water down) the amount of time you spend feeling sorry for yourself or hanging on to the trauma. The longer you delay adding the sugar and water to the lemons life hands you, the longer it will take you to move forward and enjoy the lemonade.

There is an old parable that really brings home this point:

One day a farmer's donkey fell into a deep well.

The donkey cried for hours as the farmer tried to figure out what to do. Finally, he decided the animal was old, and the well needed to be covered up anyway; it just wasn't worth it to retrieve the donkey.

He invited all his neighbors to come over and help him. They all grabbed a shovel and began to shovel dirt into the well, covering up the donkey.

At first, the donkey didn't realize what was happening and cried horribly. Then, to everyone's amazement he quieted down. A few shovel loads later, the farmer finally looked down into the well. He was astonished at what he saw. With each shovel of dirt that hit his back, the donkey was doing something amazing.

He would shake the dirt off his back, and take a step up. As the farmer's neighbors continued to shovel dirt on top of the animal, he would shake it off and take another step up. Pretty soon, the donkey stepped up over the edge of the well and happily trotted off!

MORAL OF THE STORY:

- Life is going to throw dirt on you (hand you lemons)
- Each trouble you face is a stepping stone (becomes part of the lemonade)
- We can get out of the deepest wells just by never giving up (focusing on the sweetness and the solutions)
- The trick is to shake the dirt off and take a step up (find the sweetness in the situation and dilute your fear, crying, drama)
- Life will always throw stones in the path of your success, but you get to decide if you are going to build a wall or a bridge

In her song entitled "Shake It Off", Taylor Swift introduced a sensational new version of this very old parable. There is no doubt in my mind that celebrities like Taylor Swift deal with very negative feedback on a daily basis. No matter how dynamic and successful this very talented young woman has been, she gets criticized. The nice thing for her is that she can write a song about her lemons, make millions of dollars off that song, and smile at her critics all the way to the bank. You go girl!

What about the rest of us? How does the average person overcome these adversities and critics?

I mentioned earlier that this was the second time I had to write this chapter. In writing this book, I had hit a wall with two chapters. I was having trouble getting my message conveyed exactly the way I wanted. There is just something about putting thoughts into the printed word that makes you feel like you have to get it perfect the first time or it won't be effective.

On the last week of a multi-week speaking swing, I was checking into my hotel. I noticed there was a family with two or three children checking in next to me. After signing the hotel form and getting my key, I was waiting for them to retrieve my fax. I looked down and noticed a little girl (maybe two or three years old), standing next to my briefcase and purse with an empty Coke bottle in her hand. I didn't think anything about it.

I headed off to my room, threw my purse on the bed, sat down, and ate the dinner I had picked up on my way to the hotel.

About an hour later, I grabbed my purse and pulled out my laptop. It was drenched in soda. Apparently that little girl had poured her Coke into my purse, and my laptop had been laying in a purse full of liquid for over an hour.

I immediately started drying it off and opened the lid to dry off the inside. The computer was in sleep mode, so when I opened the lid, it started up the computer and shorted out everything. The computer was now officially dead. All of my training PowerPoint presentations, my corporate accounting, all of the files for the girls I was coaching and…this book were no longer accessible. When I began to think about everything that was on that computer, my heart sank.

I wasn't due to be back home for another week, so I was unable to take the computer somewhere to see if the hard drive could be retrieved. For three more days I had to present a six-hour seminar without my computer and projector.

Interestingly enough, the two chapters that I was stuck on were now completely gone! One of those two chapters was, "When Life Gives You Lemons…"

"Did you have it backed up?" Every single person asked me that question. The answer was, "Sort of." All of my training PowerPoint presentations were backed up. The foreword and first four chapters of the book that were completed had been sent to my publisher – so she sent those back. But the remaining chapters that I was working on, massaging, processing, and trying to finish had not been backed up in their current format.

Irony at it's best. I told you earlier that God has a sense of humor!

But wait, it gets better. A few days after this accident, my publisher gave me a deadline for having the book completed to reach our desired promotion date. I now had exactly one month to complete the remaining five chapters.

I immediately thought, "Oh great. Not only was I stuck on those two chapters, now I have to completely re-write what I had already written *and* complete the entire book in one month."

One of my friends wrote and asked me this question. "How many tears have you shed over this?" I immediately wrote back and said, "None." I thought that was the strangest question. I truly did not understand how crying over this issue was going to help the situation.

I was *already* looking for the sugar and water. I was already assuming that there was going to be a sweet spot and I needed to immediately dilute this trauma so I could turn my focus back to finishing the book and reaching my deadline.

So where is the sugar you ask? Check this out:

First, with those two roadblock chapters completely gone, I was no longer staring at words that were not inspiring me. As a result of the fried computer, I now had a current real life example to write about. I now had a fresh page, fresh ideas, and a new deadline (which always motivates me – I work well under pressure). I re-wrote those two lost chapters in one day, to completion!

Second, when I called Apple Care, the customer service representative pulled up my serial number and said, "Wait a minute. There is a message connected to your computer's serial number. It says that this computer qualifies for a new logic board at no cost regardless of the cause of the damage."

"So let me get this straight. Even though the computer is not under warranty, I can get a free logic board and possibly get the computer operating again?"

Although the new logic board did not resolve the issue and I was unable to recover the hard drive, I was able to sell the fried computer with the new logic board for $415 which helped pay for the brand new computer with a new warranty! Hmm, sugar anyone?

In an earlier chapter I shared the comments I had received from my friends when I asked them what they felt had aided me in achieving my successes. Resilience and perseverance were on the list. Here I was writing a chapter about resilience and perseverance when I was tested one more time… "Here's Your Lemon!"

Lemons come in all shapes, sizes, and styles. For some people, a lemon gets served up as another person saying or doing something to hurt their feelings. It can be accidents, or losing a sporting event, pageant or job. For others, it can come in the form of losing a relationship or loved one.

No matter what kind of lemon life hands you, the experience can be embarrassing, painful, and for some, debilitating.

It is certainly not my intent to suggest that all of life's challenges are as easy to get over as losing a computer. There are, in fact, some events or challenges in life that can test you down to your very core.

I do know that every single human being faces lemons or difficult problems over the course of their lifetime. Some face personal life problems while others deal with career problems.

The fascinating truth is that people handle these problems very differently. Some people run away from their problems, hoping they can avoid the pain. But running away from problems is probably the worst choice you could make when it comes to dealing with life's lemons.

There are other people who cling to lemons or problems forever. They refuse to look for the sugar or to add the water to their pitcher of lemon juice. They choose to live in misery, talking about their lemons, showing their lemons to everyone, telling the story of how life handed them their lemons over and over.

This too is not healthy. It's one thing to have great memories and celebrate those memories. It's another to make your lemons the subject of your communications the majority of the time. If a person lingers too long clinging to their lemons, that behavior could easily become a "victim mentality".

One of the most inspiring examples of creating "sugar" and "watering down the trauma" to make it manageable, is the story of John Walsh. For those of you who are not familiar, John Walsh gained publicity after his six-year-old son, Adam Walsh, was kidnapped and murdered in 1981. Walsh and others had successfully advocated Congress for the creation of the National Center for Missing and Exploited Children.

In 1988, Walsh became the host for the television show, *America's Most Wanted*. This show was credited with capturing more than 1,200 fugitives wanted for serious crimes including murder, rape, kidnapping, child molestation, white-collar crime, organized crime, armed robbery, gang violence, and terrorism.

What an incredible testimony of creating something "sweet" out of such a tragedy. However, in thinking back to the many times I watched John Walsh on his TV shows or on interviews, I rarely heard him talk about his son's death as much as he talked about what he was doing more recently. He had let it go and moved on (although I'm sure he ever forgot).

In learning how to get better at finding the sugar and watering down your sour lemonade, consider these suggestions:

1. **Put the oxygen mask on yourself first.** As I mentioned in an earlier chapter, anyone who has ever taken a commercial flight knows the pre-flight announcements the flight attendants always make. One of the comments they always make is, "In case of loss of cabin pressure, oxygen masks will drop from above you. Apply the mask over your nose and mouth, placing the elastic strap over your head, and tighten by pulling the straps on each side of the mask. Please apply the mask to yourself before attempting to assist those around you."

   Why? If you are passed out on the floor of the airplane because you can't breathe, just exactly who do you plan to help?

   The single most important thing you must do when dealing with any lemon life hands you, is put the oxygen mask on yourself first. Take care of you first. You cannot resolve conflict, fix problems, or have enough fight for the long-haul of any trauma if you become sick, depressed or unable to think clearly.

   Also, if you are tired, angry and/or depressed, it's so much more difficult to find the "sweetness" or the positives in any situation.

2. **Improve your emotional intelligence**. When life hands you lemons (regardless if the lemon is another person or a situation), it is imperative that you control your emotional responses — do not over-react. Doing so could cause you to say or do things that you might regret later. I was recently watching a documentary about a young farmer in Iowa who ended up buried alive in a very large corn bin. He survived for over two hours due to a couple of major factors. First, he had on a special mask that protected his face and kept the corn from suffocating him. Secondly, and more important, his mother had trained her children to never, ever panic. She would tell them, "If we're at the fair and you get lost, don't panic. Panic will kill you before anything else." He was able to calm his thinking, focus on survival, and by doing so, he slowed his breathing and heart rate. This is what saved his life.

Another great example of this is when people compete in sports or pageants and don't win. For them, this is a lemon and I've seen countless examples of competitors and their parents exhibit a lack of emotional intelligence by publicly blaming everyone and everything else, and not taking any responsibility for the loss themselves.

Emotional intelligence tops the list as a key factor in watering down the trauma and drama so you can get on with making your lemonade.

3. **Don't get emotionally attached to an outcome**. When you are emotionally attached to the outcome of anything, it becomes very difficult to maintain your emotional intelligence when you need to adjust or change that outcome. This is especially true when you have unrealistic expectations, and those expectations aren't met. Suddenly you will find yourself emotional and upset because you didn't get the outcome you expected. Set goals, make plans, and

then move forward knowing that your plans may come together, or they may not.

4. **Face the facts.** So often, people have unrealistic expectations of other people or life situations. Once life hands you lemons, the best course of action is to simply accept what has happened and move on to the recovery or solution. Sitting around wishing that the situation hadn't happened or didn't exist will not help you.

5. **Do your due diligence.** When something happens in your life (much like my laptop getting fried by a little girl and a Coke), rather than fall apart and feeling sorry for yourself, start doing research. Had I not made phone calls and inquiries, I would not have found out about the free logic board replacement. In the business world, we call that due diligence… research. Don't assume anything! Get the facts and find out what your options are.

   If your lemon involves another person, you must get the facts from that person. Ask them what they meant, or why they said/did what they said/did. Stop jumping to conclusions, making assumptions or deciding exactly why people did what they did without first giving them the opportunity to explain.

6. **Avoid analysis paralysis.** Sometimes when people start doing their research (doing their due diligence), and they come up with options, they will then get stuck in analysis. Thinking and overthinking and reviewing and thinking. The purpose of doing research is to provide you with enough information to make an educated decision. Quite often that educated decision will simply have to be based on a hunch, a feeling, a risk. One thing I know for sure is that successful people are risk takers. Calculated risks of course, but risk takers nonetheless. Sometimes they win, and sometimes their risk doesn't pay off. But the most

important thing to note is that you must look at the overall picture. Are your payoffs greater than your losses? If so, you are moving forward!

7. **Make a game plan for your next steps.** No matter what kind of lemon life hands you, you are the only person who can develop a plan to move forward. You must evaluate your research, compare your options, and then create a plan of action. What is it going to take to overcome it, fix it, repair it, or move around, over or under it? Then... take action! Do something even if it's wrong, but you must move forward and adjust as you go.

8. **Don't compare your lifestyle with others.** Unless you are prepared to compare your work ethic, action steps, commitment level, and sacrifices to other people, then you absolutely should NOT compare your lifestyle or successes to other people. If you don't get the same results as other people, then you have to be willing to step back and make an honest evaluation of the work or commitment you had going in. Every single person brings different talents to the table. Your talents may take you farther in another field, so you can't compare yourself to others.

9. **Let go of what you can't change.** Often people cling to situations much longer than they should; investing entirely too much time trying to change a situation or outcome when that time would be better spent moving forward. When you are overwhelmed with issues, the first thing to do is learn to let go of the things you simply cannot change. Doing otherwise takes away energy from problems you can actually fix.

   • Let go of your past. Let go of your mistakes. Learn from them, but let them go! Problems in your past will often come to a better resolution when you work towards a better future, even if that just means you begin to realize that those mistakes don't define you.

- Let go of that friend that refuses to forgive you for whatever it is you did. Instead, focus on solving your other problems and work on making the rest of your life and actions as good as they can be.

10. **Be ready to make some sacrifices**. In order to come out of negative situations or survive bad relations, you may have to make sacrifices. Always look at things long-term. You may have to give up things for a short period of time, in order to have what you truly want or need later on, and you will have to be ready to make those sacrifices.

Successful women do not drink sour lemonade. They immediately start looking for the sugar (the sweetness in the situation), and they water down the trauma (they don't go on and on about the situation). As a result, they are able to enjoy the refreshment of a wonderful, cool glass of lemonade in spite of the lemons that life hands them.

YOUR MOXIE MISSION
(Should You Choose To Accept It)

1. Do some self-discovery. Think about the lemons that life has handed you (past relationships, financial hardships, lost opportunities, disappointments, etc.). Now, be really honest with yourself. Are you still walking around with any of those lemons, clinging to the trauma and drama? If you answered "Yes, but…" let me stop you right there. The answer is simply YES. There is no "but" or "however". It's time to start looking for the sugar (or sweetness) and focusing on that instead. It's time to water down that trauma or drama and let it go! Let me assure you that your friends will grow weary of hearing about it!

2. The next time life hands you a lemon, *and* before you start blaming someone or something else for the lemon, stop and ask yourself these questions (be really honest with yourself when you are searching for the answers):

    *   What could I have done (if anything) to avoid this situation?

    *   What positive lesson can I learn from this situation?

    *   Did I have unrealistic expectations going into this situation?

    *   Have I started looking for the sugar yet (the sweetness in the situation)? If yes, good for you. If no, what the heck are you waiting for… start looking!

    *   Have I gone through the list of suggestions outlined at the end of this chapter? If yes, awesome! If no, start right now.

CHAPTER 7

Conflict Is Not a Dirty Word

Myth #6
*If You Can't Say
Anything Nice,
Don't Say
Anything at All*

I'm sure just reading the title of this chapter has already created conflict and stress for some readers. I really don't know many people who actually like conflict.

But I do know that conflict exists and it does make living in peace extremely difficult. The challenge is not always the conflict itself. The problem is that most women don't like and avoid conflict, and/or won't engage in conflict resolution. I believe the reason is that women do not embrace this quote:

Moxie Minute:
*The purpose of argument is not victory,
but understanding.*

It took me decades to finally understand that talking *through* disagreements, hurt feelings, or conflicts was going to be necessary to allow me to hear both sides of an issue before forming my conclusion, and to prevent me from making inaccurate assumptions or placing blame where it didn't belong.

This begs the question... why are women so afraid or unwilling to engage in efforts to resolve conflict?

In pondering this question, I thought back to my childhood and the lessons I was taught as a young girl. These are the same lessons that I'm sure many of you were taught as well, even though you may not have realized it at the time.

I can remember playing Barbies with my friends on the breezeway in Emporia, Kansas. We had the Barbie Dream House, a Barbie closet full of Barbie clothes, and I even had a Barbie sports car. We would play for hours, dressing and redressing our dolls, and creating one make-believe scenario after another.

Every once in a while, my friend and I would get into an argument over whose Barbie was going to drive the Barbie sports car (don't laugh...those were very important issues at that time in our lives). The squabble would begin and it would get louder until my mother would come out to the breezeway, put her hands on her hips, and begin "the speech" I had heard countless times before.

"If you and your little friend can't get along, I'm going to send your friend home!"

There it was. The lesson! "If you can't get along, all the time, you don't get to play." It's a lesson that many young women are still taught today. Unfortunately, it is a lesson that women brought into their adult lives, their jobs, their relationships, their sports, and their friendships. Many women truly believe that if they don't get along with everyone in every setting, they could lose their job, friendships, or support groups.

Then I started thinking about young boys, how they play, and the lessons they are taught. Young boys often participate on youth sports leagues – track, basketball, baseball, soccer, rodeo, and football. I've watched as they literally kick, push, shove, and attack each other during the game. In fact, it can get intensely competitive. After the game is over, the players line up in two lines and give each other high-fives while congratulating the winners. Then, the coaches or the parents take the kids for pizza or ice cream.

I don't know about you, but my momma never took my friend and me for pizza or ice cream after we had a squabble over the Barbie car. NEVER!

Young boys are taught to work as a team, while seeking individual ranking within the sport. They are taught to fight, compete, push and shove, and when it's all over you get over it. They too bring that lesson into their adult lives. They will have a disagreement with a co-worker or competitor and quite often after the argument or disagreement is over, they will go to lunch or grab a beer together and go home. I agree this may not be the case in 100% of the situations, but I'm relatively positive men are better at this than women.

When women have a disagreement or conflict, they will talk to everyone about it *except* the one person who can answer the questions, explain their side of the conflict, or do anything about it. Then women will pass the conflict down through their lineage. Their great grandchildren will know about the conflict decades later. Women are simply not good at addressing concerns head-on and tend to hold grudges.

I like to explain conflict using this analogy:

Have you ever seen a child with a splinter in their hand? They will come to you with their hand stretched out, demanding that you fix it. With a loving smile on your face, you say, "Sure, let me get that out for you." The child is *all about* you removing the splinter until…you whip out the needle. Almost immediately the child will pull their little hand back and exclaim, "NO, it's all right now!" Why?

Because the child does a quick assessment simply based on what they see, and makes the decision that you will cause more pain with the needle than is being caused by the splinter. The child's split second decision is based on past experiences. For example, maybe the child has had you dig out a splinter before using a needle and it did *not* go well...it was painful. Maybe the last time the child had a splinter, someone else took it out and they simply were not as gentle as you might be. Maybe the child remembers their last trip to the doctor's office where they had a shot with a needle and your needle reminds them of that experience. Or maybe it is simply fear of the unknown.

Of course, there is another possible reason. The child may have a low threshold for pain, and just knows that the process of removing the splinter is going to hurt. So the child decides to live with the "lesser" pain, or so they perceive. Regardless the reason, the child assumes that taking the splinter out is going to be more painful than leaving the splinter in.

Here's the problem with that plan.

Can a splinter work itself out? Yes, of course. Does a splinter work itself out *most* of the time? I'm sure most people would agree that unfortunately the answer is no. In most cases a splinter stays tight in the skin, gets infected, festers, and becomes a much bigger issue than if you had simply addressed it to begin with.

In conflict situations, the similarities to the splinter analogy are many. Let's take a look at April and Susan. In this example, the splinter represents conflict and the needle represents attempts at conflict resolution.

After several interactions, April becomes frustrated with Susan's insults during departmental meetings. The insults are offensive and April feels that Susan "should know better and refrain from the behavior." But the comments keep coming.

After brewing and stewing about the situation, April goes to her boss for advice (she metaphorically sticks her hand out and asks her boss to "fix" the problem and reduce the discomfort of the situation).

After listening to her concerns, April's boss suggests that she go directly to Susan to calmly and professionally discuss her concerns and set a boundary. Immediately April says, "Oh my, I wouldn't be comfortable doing that." (When hearing that she would need to address the situation directly — the "needle" — April pulls her hand back in and says, "No, it's all right now!") Why?

Because April does a quick assessment simply based on what she *thinks* might happen, and makes the decision that talking directly to Susan will cause more pain than leaving the conflict in place and just living with the insults.

As we discussed with the child and splinter, that split second decision is based on past experiences. For example, maybe April has tried to talk with Susan about an issue before and it did *not* go well...it was painful. Maybe the last time April had a conflict with someone different, that person attacked her instead of addressing the situation calmly and professionally, and now she assumes everyone will respond the same way. Maybe April has watched other people try to resolve conflict without success. Or maybe it is simply the fear of the unknown. Regardless the reason, April assumes that talking to Susan about her concerns is going to be painful.

Maybe April simply does not know *how* to set boundaries or share her concerns calmly and professionally. Let's face it, learning how to work with people without wanting to kill them is not a class we can take in college.

Of course, there is another possible reason. April may be a Lamb personality whose biggest fear is conflict, and therefore has a low threshold for dealing with conflict. Instead, April decides to live with the "lesser" pain, or so she perceives.

This reminds me of the old saying, "better to dance with the devil you know than the devil you don't." When it comes to conflict, most women (well let's face it, most people) believe it is better to deal with a person or choose an option/solution they know (even if it is not what they would most like) than it is to deal with someone they know nothing about or an option with which they have no experience. In other words, known things are to be preferred over the unknown — even if they are not ideal.

In both cases, leaving the splinter in place *may* be less painful in the short run, but can certainly be more painful in the long run. In the case of conflict, the thought of having to face someone with your concerns and thoughts, or to have to set a boundary can be traumatic. However, if April has to be subjected to Susan's public insults day after day on her job, she will become angry, resentful and may even leave a great job because she never spoke up.

Personality certainly plays a huge role in the area of conflict. Introverted personalities (Lambs and Owls) who are normally quieter may not be as quick to stand up for themselves or address concerns. They may fear not being able to hold their own with a stronger personality so they simply do not engage in discussions to possibly resolve conflict.

How can you even try to resolve a conflict when one person won't participate? You can't! Thus, conflict lingers, hangs around and interferes with relationships.

Because it has been estimated that 69% of our population are Lamb personalities, whose biggest fear is conflict, it makes sense why so many people are in conflict with each other (why so many people have chosen to keep the splinter in place rather than have it removed by attempting to discuss differences).

This leads to my all time favorite Moxie minute:

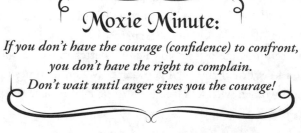

Moxie Minute:

If you don't have the courage (confidence) to confront,
you don't have the right to complain.
Don't wait until anger gives you the courage!

In this quote, the word confront does not mean to be confrontational. It means if you don't have the courage or confidence to address a situation (to talk through a conflict with the person involved, to express how you feel about something, or to set a boundary) then you really don't have the right to complain about it, to *anyone*. Don't talk about it to everyone else in your office, on your team, or in your pageant circles. And whatever you do, don't plaster it all over Facebook, Twitter, or LinkedIn.

Unfortunately, what happens most often is people who do not have the courage to *calmly* and *professionally* address a situation will brew and stew, work themselves into a frenzy and then verbally "show up and throw up" on people. They wait until anger gives them the courage to say something, and by then it is often too late to control their emotions. When this happens, you cross over into the passive-aggressive communication style. Now, even if the other person did something that was considered inappropriate or offensive, *you* may end up losing the respect of others because of the way you handled (or didn't handle) the conflict.

Here is a great example of what I'm talking about.

Several years ago I bought a home in the St. Louis area, and after a short period of time I decided that I wanted to live in Florida for at least half of the year. I rented a townhouse in St. Petersburg, Florida and retained ownership of the St. Louis house.

Because I didn't want the Missouri house sitting vacant for six months, and because I planned to live in that house part of the year, I decided to find a roommate. It was a great deal for her as she had the house to herself half of the year and only had to pay half the costs. It was a great deal for me because someone was in the house to keep an eye on it and it offset some of my costs.

A few months after I went to Florida, I decided to sell a new treadmill I had in the basement of the Missouri house. Because I was in Florida, it wasn't being used, but running an ad for the treadmill and selling it in Missouri was going to be a challenge.

I contacted my roommate and explained what I wanted to do. I then asked her if she would be comfortable allowing people into the home to see the treadmill and if it sold, collecting the money on my behalf. She thought for a very brief moment and then said, "Sure, no problem," in a very upbeat non-confrontational tone.

With the green light from my roommate, I ran the ad, we set up appointments for people to see the treadmill, and it eventually sold. I thanked her for helping me with the transaction and she again said, "No problem. Glad I could help."

About three weeks later, I received a scathing letter in the mail from my roommate. She proceeded to inform me that I had been extremely rude for even asking her to take care of the treadmill situation and that she didn't appreciate it at all!

WOW! That came straight out of nowhere. I had no idea that was how she felt, primarily because *she* had led me to believe that it would not be a problem to help me with the request.

I had respected her enough to call and ask if she would be comfortable with it. She had every opportunity to tell me, "No." I would have respected her response and figured out another solution for selling the treadmill.

But instead, she told me it would not be a problem, when apparently it was a problem. That is what we call passive behavior/communication. Then she waited until anger gave her the courage and she unloaded on me. That is what we call passive-aggressive behavior/communication. By definition, passive-aggressive behavior is when a person is "outwardly nice, but inwardly hostile."

Because she didn't have the courage to tell me up front that she was not comfortable with my request, she agreed to it. Then from that moment on she was brewing and stewing about how rude it was for *me* to make that request. She worked herself into a frenzy until she finally blew up in a letter to me. She didn't even have the courage to do it in a phone call.

Not once in her letter did she take responsibility for telling me it would be okay or for not setting a boundary with me on that original phone call. Instead, she placed 100% of the blame on me for even asking.

I am positive that every person reading this chapter has either been on the receiving end of an encounter like this one, or has been the person who said, "Sure that's fine," and then blew up on someone later.

I see this sort of situation happen daily, women who simply do not have the confidence to stand up for their own rights. They don't set boundaries, they don't communicate what they are thinking, or they don't share their concerns. Then, if you don't handle the situation the way they want, they get angry and let you have it! I also believe, however, that there may be another culprit.

This leads us to Myth #6: *If you can't say anything nice, don't say anything at all!*

This myth, while in theory makes a great deal of sense, has single-handedly turned women into a passive-aggressive hot mess.

This age-old phrase has been handed down for decades without any real explanation of what it meant. Clearly, if you're at a party where people are talking about someone, if you can't say anything nice about the person you should probably refrain from sharing.

Unfortunately, I believe that this old adage has been taken out of context on more than one occasion and used as an excuse to avoid conflict. I can just hear April (from our example earlier in the chapter) having this internal dialogue…

"I just hate how Susan speaks to me in front of other people. I just want to tell her off and let her know how that makes me feel. But my mom always said, 'If you can't say something nice, don't say anything at all.' I know if I try to talk to her about this it isn't going to be nice. So I'll just keep silent about it. I'll just have to tolerate her behavior."

I do not believe this old adage meant you should stand by and allow people to aggressively attack you, humiliate you, or abuse your rights.

By definition, assertive communication is "standing up for your rights, without infringing on the rights of others." I teach every day the importance of learning how to be an assertive communicator. Obviously, in order to do that, you must likewise learn how to calmly and professionally stand up for your own rights. This requires speaking up, expressing your concerns with behaviors, and setting boundaries to protect yourself.

I think it's time to change this old adage so it makes better sense.

"If you can't say something NICELY, don't say anything at all."

There now! Doesn't that make a world of difference! Now it's very clear that you *can* stand up for yourself, set boundaries, share concerns or express dissatisfactions, as long as you can do it calmly, professionally and assertively.

Voila! Problem solved! Well not completely...there's still another problem.

Probably the hardest part about becoming an assertive communicator, who has the confidence to stand your ground calmly and professionally, is that the person receiving your message may still think you are not being nice, or that you are aggressive and rude.

Recently I had a huge epiphany. When women take my training to heart and actually stand up for themselves, many times they are called a bully or a bitch. It's no wonder women are afraid to assertively speak up, stand up, and set boundaries. They're punished or reprimanded, especially by other women, when they do it.

With the whole world taking everything personally, it seems we have simply stopped *listening* assertively or stepping back to look at the bigger picture. We assume motives, we assume what people meant, we're "sure she did that to me," and with social media taking over communications it isn't getting any better.

I have two Facebook advice pages – one for my professional speaker page and one for the Rodeo Queen coaching that I do. On both of these pages I provide advice, stories, articles, and motivational quotes. On my "Queens In Jeans" Facebook page, I also share what I lovingly call "soapbox moments" where I address hardcore issues and attitudes in the industry. I think it's fair to say that most authors would tell you the things they write about are inspired by events they witness or experience. I'm no different. I write articles on my page based on behaviors I witness, or concerns that people in the industry will call and share with me. Because I'm not affiliated with any one organization, I feel that I can speak from a neutral standpoint. When I write these special articles, I never mention names, pageants, states or individual situations. In fact, I usually make up stories to make my point.

It never fails, however, that women will read something I write, something that *every* young woman needs to hear and learn from, and they make the choice to claim and internalize it. They *choose* to take it personally and they will attack me for humiliating them in public. Not once do they call me and ask for clarification; not once do they call and ask what my motive was; not once do they ask if I was actually referring to them; not once do they just say, "I really didn't appreciate what I think you did." They just turn the knife so they can get even without ever stopping to think that they *might* be wrong.

Wow — so now what do we do? Simply put, grow a thick skin! In order to be an assertive communicator, to stand up for your rights (even if you do it calmly and professionally), it will require that you learn how to keep your head held high even if they call you a bitch. Always remember that you may be the only person who will stand up for you.

I do have to take just a moment and address an important issue — learn to pick your battles. Not every issue needs to be addressed. Sometimes when we *choose* to get our feelings hurt we don't step back to think whether or not this issue really does negatively affect us before taking action. The next time someone says or does something that you *choose* to be offended by before you have any facts, use this method to determine if you need to pick the battle or if you should let it go. Ask yourself this question:

Does "this" (person, comment, situation, event) negatively affect me...

1. Financially (has it taken money out of my pocket)?
2. Physically (did it cause me physical harm – did they bite me, slap me, kick me or ask me to carry something too heavy for me)?

    NOTE: Many times women will tell me "Yes, it upset me and caused me stress." That is an emotional response, not a physical one. Do not pick battles over emotional issues, you may win the battle and lose the war.
3. Professionally (did it cost me a promotion, cost me credibility, etc.)?

If the answer is "No, No, No," – LET IT GO! Just for the record, this means really let it go. Don't hold a grudge; don't keep bringing it up; don't keep brewing and stewing about it!

If the answer to one of the questions is "Yes," then you must ask yourself, "How?" Once you have that answer, you will know exactly the issue that needs to be addressed rather than talking about how unfair it is, or "how it makes you feel" (especially in the workplace).

Unfortunately, this jumping to conclusions and turning the knife issue happens in all areas of our lives, career and social. We jump to conclusions, assume the worst in every situation, don't ask for clarification or set boundaries. We just go for the jugular and turn the knife.

To help with learning how to control your runaway emotions that are jumping to conclusions, start practicing this advice.

Moxie Minute:

Always assume the best until you know the worst.

This means always assume the best case scenario until you know for sure what the truth is or what really happened. This helps you to prevent jumping to conclusions and finding out you were wrong.

When I'm faced with someone jumping to conclusions about something I've said or done, I utilize the assertive communication technique entitled Negative Inquiry. I will contact the person direct with the intention of resolving the conflict and ask this question:

"I may be misreading the signals, but I get the sense that I may have offended you. Have I said or done something to offend you? Maybe I owe you an apology."

OMG! (*Enter sarcasm here*) God forbid that I would address an issue directly with the person who is apparently upset with me. What was I thinking trying to resolve a conflict? How utterly rude of me to reach out to that person (instead of talking about him/her to everyone I come in contact with) to find out what has happened, or why they are upset! I'm such a bully! (*Sarcasm complete.*)

I can honestly tell you I have rarely had a man behave that way. I can talk to a man about a conflict or disagreement and in a couple of days we can pick up and move on. It's refreshing actually. However, as I said earlier, as long as women continue to take everything personally, it becomes very difficult to be a confident, assertive communicator.

As a society, we spend hundreds of thousands of dollars for counselors so they can teach us how to communicate with each other. Marriage counselors, relationship counselors, and/or personal counselors. In most of those counseling sessions, the counselor will encourage the participants to talk to each other about how it makes them feel, or how it affects them.

Wouldn't it just be easier (and cheaper) if we could work on learning how to address conflict with each other, stop taking things personally, learn how to listen assertively (hear what the other person is saying without taking it personally) and quit assuming what the other person meant?

The answer is, "YES, it would be easier." But until we as women can stop taking everything so personally and attacking each other, nothing will change.

My father taught me a very valuable lesson years ago through one of my favorite parables. Let me share that with you:

The Parable Of the Bird and the Cow

There was a bird that lived in Canada. One winter he announced to the other birds, "I'm not flying south for the winter. I'm staying right here!" All the other birds said he was crazy, but he answered, "You're the ones that are crazy. You'll get down south, turn around and fly right back up here again next year. What's the point?"

The other birds took to flight and left him behind.

Wondering what winter in Canada would be like, the lone bird was pleasantly surprised at the stretch of Indian summer that lingered long into the fall. "Aha!" he said to himself, "I was right to stay. This is wonderful!"

But then, winter hit full force in the middle of December. Shuddering in the cold the silly bird finally realized, "I must hurry and leave before I freeze to death!"

He took to flight and made it as far as Montana. There, in mid-air, he froze up and tumbled to the ground, landing in a farmer's barnyard. "Oh, what a stupid bird I am," he moaned to himself. "I should've flown south with all the other birds, but now I am about to die."

Just then a cow in the barnyard strolled past the fallen bird and without realizing it dropped a big cow-plop right on top of him! "Oh, this is just great," mumbled the buried bird. "It's not bad enough that I'm about to die; now I'm covered with cow manure!"

But then he noticed something he had not expected. The warmth of the plop actually began to thaw him out and restore him to life. "Why, what do you know about that?" said the bird. "This ain't so bad after all!" Then he began chirping and singing under the pile of cow plop.

Meanwhile, the barnyard cat was passing by and heard the sound of singing coming from the pile. Curious as a cat can be, he pawed around in the pile and uncovered the thawed bird. Their eyes met, there was a silent moment of suspense, and then the cat ate the bird.

THE MORAL OF THE STORY

- **First,** not everyone who craps on you is your enemy
- **Second,** not everyone who digs you out of the crap is your friend
- **Third,** when you get dumped on, it is sometimes best to keep your mouth shut

Ladies, I truly believe the single most important lesson a woman with Moxie needs to learn is how to tell the difference between an enemy and an ally.

- Just because someone disagrees with you, does not mean they hate you.

- Just because someone gets angry at you, doesn't mean they hate you.
- Just because someone writes something that seems really close to home, does not mean they were writing about you. This is like when you're sitting in church, the minister is preaching and you just KNOW he is talking right at you. If you are feeling guilty about something that has been said, this *ally* just gave you an opportunity to look at yourself and grow – don't waste it!
- Just because someone shares a concern or sets a boundary with you, does not mean they hate or disrespect you. It may mean they also respect themselves enough to set a boundary that *you* stepped over.
- If you are avoiding people because of a conflict or disagreement, it is usually because you left the splinter in to avoid the "assumed" pain. How's that working for you?

It's time to grow up and learn how to assertively stand up for your rights, without infringing on the rights of others. Learn to listen without prejudice, discuss with an open mind, and find a win-win solution so that both parties walk away feeling like the conflict resolution was a success.

Just to be clear, there are women out there, like me, who are not so easily offended and/or who are willing to talk through conflict. Those are the professional, successful women with Moxie I'm referring to who kick these myths and lies to the curb!

YOUR MOXIE MISSION
(Should You Choose to Accept It)

1. First, and most important, learn how to QTIP everything!
   a. **Q**uit **T**aking **I**t **P**ersonally
2. Embrace this Moxie Minute:
   a. Always assume the BEST until you know the WORST!
   b. Give the benefit of the doubt in a situation until you know, for a fact, the worst-case scenario.
3. Let's talk through Conflict!
   a. Listen for and watch (nonverbals) what is felt, as well as what is being said
   b. Remember – "The purpose of argument is not victory, but understanding!" Make conflict resolution the priority, instead of focusing on winning or "being right."
   c. Focus on the "here and now." While you may need to reference a past situation as an example, do not get stuck digging up old wounds for the purpose of turning the knife
   d. Pick your battles. Practice using the technique outlined in this chapter to determine if you *should* pick a battle. Step back, look at the big picture and determine how the comment, person, or event really affected you. If you hear yourself say, "Well it's the principle of the thing," STOP! Those words are the devil and you are about to pick a battle for the wrong reason!
   e. Be willing to forgive. Everyone makes mistakes – even you! If you want others to forgive you, then you must lead by example.

CHAPTER 8

What People See Is What They Think They Are Getting

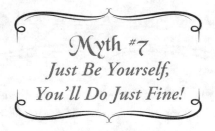

Myth #7
*Just Be Yourself,
You'll Do Just Fine!*

I've always found it incredibly interesting in any situation where you are interviewing for or being judged for selection as the best candidate, that people always say, "Just be yourself, you'll do just fine!"

As with every other chapter in this book, I'm going to say that yes, in theory, this makes sense and should be the way to succeed.

Unfortunately, anyone reading this book knows that just "being yourself" rarely gets you the job, wins the pageant, or gets you accepted.

This realization started for me when I was in high school. Every day during the summers, I would ride my bicycle about five miles to where we kept our horses. Then I would groom, saddle, ride for hours, unsaddle, feed, buck bales of hay and then ride my bicycle another five miles back home. My point being that I was not a lazy teenager who sat around and watched TV. I was very physically active.

Nevertheless, in high school where many of my female peers were a size two through six, I was a size ten…not fat, but certainly stocky. Unfortunately, in high school, when you are larger than your peers, you are often viewed as fat and lazy anyway.

This supports the first Moxie Minute and title of this chapter:

Moxie Minute:
What people see is what they think they're getting!

Whether you like it or not, when people look at you, they will form opinions or jump to conclusions about you, your socio-economic status, level of education (vs. knowledge), successes, commitment levels, and more.

The year I won Miss Rodeo Kansas I realized pretty quickly that "just being myself" wasn't remotely going to be enough to be competitive at the national level. The Kansas titleholder the year before me became the first Miss Rodeo Kansas to bring home the Miss Rodeo America crown. No pressure, right?

After being crowned Miss Rodeo Kansas, I had the opportunity to spend the weekend at her home, working with her to get some much needed assistance as I prepared to go to the national pageant.

To this day, I can still clearly remember arriving at her home. I pulled into the driveway, got out of the car and said hello to her mother who was standing at the front door. While I can't guarantee exactly what she said, the only thing I can remember her saying was, "Well, I can tell you right now that if you can't get your teeth straightened and lose thirty pounds in the next six months, you might as well not even go to the Miss Rodeo America pageant!"

There it was. The first time in my life that I had regretted begging my mother to forego the braces when I was in seventh grade! It was right at this very moment I learned that "just being myself" was not going to get the job done.

As I've told this story over the years, it's about here that people will interject their comments about how rude this woman was and how she should have been more encouraging to a young woman. Everyone seems to think that she was a bully to me. To be honest, I did get my feelings hurt, but only for a very brief amount of time. Women with Moxie don't internalize comments or take things personally for long. We are able to control our emotions, hear the message for what it's worth, digest the information, and then apply it as we deem appropriate.

The way I looked at it, I was the predecessor to the first Kansas queen to bring home the national title and I wasn't about to follow that up by being someone who didn't at least put an effort into my year as her replacement. Not only that, they must have done *something* right to bring home the Miss Rodeo America crown, so who was I to get all bent out of shape when I was the one who asked for their help to begin with?

After that weekend, I came home ready to do everything within my means to make the changes she had suggested. Looking back, I doubt when her mother made that comment, she believed I would be able to act on it in such a short period of time. Then again, I'm sure she didn't realize who she was dealing with!

My sister worked as a dental assistant, and after telling her about my teeth straightening challenge, she suggested we talk to her boss. Turns out he had been working on an experimental contraption that would be a removable version of traditional braces. His invention was made of wire with a molded plastic center and a literal crank that could be used to push the teeth out and into line.

I had a need and NO budget, and the dentist had an experimental solution with no one to test it on — we were a match made in heaven. So, I became the guinea pig for his contraption. While he would check it, adjust it and make sure it was doing what it was supposed to do, my only job was to keep inflicting this excruciating pain on myself by turning the crank once a week and NOT taking the bloody thing out of my mouth when it started hurting too badly.

In the last chapter, I talked about finding the sweetness in situations. Even as painful as this story sounds, I can point out the sweetness (in case you haven't figured it out already). Even though I was under the watchful eye of a dental professional, we were moving my teeth in a bit of a record-breaking timeframe. As a result, it was painful to chew, so I only ate when necessary to maintain my health and nutrition. I was not motivated to cheat because it simply wasn't worth the discomfort. This, of course, made losing weight much easier. As a result of this invention, I was killing two birds with one crank…straightening my teeth and losing thirty pounds in six months (which by the way was still within recommended weight loss goals of two pounds per week).

This brings us to a critical question. Do women have to meet a certain physical standard to be successful?

The answer is a resounding "NO"…well in most cases!

The issue of having to change who you are to be "successful" often raises much controversy. Women will debate that they shouldn't have to be thin, drop dead gorgeous, have perfectly white teeth and have a Ph.D. to be successful. Just for the record, I couldn't agree more! Why? Because I am that person. I am the plus-size woman with no college degree who even after enduring that mouth full of pain still does not have perfect teeth (although they are drastically better than where they were before the torture chamber).

While there are certainly people who will deny you opportunities for one or more of those liabilities, a woman with Moxie simply does not let NO stop her from pushing forward.

Since I have been a plus-size woman the majority of my adult life, it has been blatantly clear to me that there can be a double standard as it relates to my credibility due to size and/or appearance. Unfortunately, people still walk around with prejudices or preconceived notions about what they see. They will pass judgment regarding your level of education (we will discuss this in the next chapter), overall beauty (are you a model?), having to wear glasses (four-eyes), weight ("if you're fat you're lazy"), tattoos (you must be in a gang or motorcycle clan), beautiful pearly whites (because clearly that makes you smarter), smoker, drinker...the list goes on and on.

As much as people don't want to admit that it's true, the reality is our society as a whole does not show the same respect to people with these "liabilities." Of all the physical judgments that society tries to place upon us, being overweight is one of the most scrutinized issues.

I'm sure we've all seen shows where the host spends a day in a fat suit and lives a day in the life of an overweight person. At the end of just one day as a plus-size person, the host has a complete "a-ha" moment and talks about how devastating it was to be treated with such disdain. I've even watched as some hosts had a complete meltdown after only one day.

The one I remember most was when Tyra Banks (international model and talk show host) took on this project. She first visited several retail stores and restaurants as her "model" self. She then went through the transformation from international model to a plus-size beauty.

We watched as she went back to the same retail stores and restaurants as a plus-size woman. By the end of her day she sat in tears and talked about how she had never experienced the rudeness and belittlement that had been directed toward her when she presented herself as a plus-size woman.

I have personally experienced the prejudice that takes place when you are a plus-size person. Unfortunately, I have also experienced people telling me, "It's all in my head." I beg to disagree!

Throughout my national and international travels, I have experienced this epidemic globally. In 2014, I was training in Australia with a dear friend and fabulous trainer. We were conducting a women's conference, spending our days empowering and motivating women to reach their full potential.

At the end of one of our training days, our driver picked us up at the hotel and off we went to the airport. Very quickly he began flirting by talking about how "lovely" we were. Unfortunately the compliment took a nosedive.

"What a nice pair of ladies and the lady in the blue is especially beautiful." My dear friend was wearing a blue jacket! It wasn't long before I clearly didn't exist in the car.

I just sat there, quietly shaking my head and thinking to myself, "Are you kidding me? HELLO…I'm sitting right here. You can certainly be attracted to anyone you want, but for the love of God do you have to shove it right in my face?"

My friend looked at me and her face said it all…she was absolutely mortified. After we had exited the car, she exclaimed, "I'm so sorry for that!"

"No need to be sorry. It wasn't your doing. Besides, he really screwed up."

"How did he screw up?" she asked.

I smiled and quipped, "Between the two of us, I'm the one who tips." (In Australia tipping is not the norm, but because it was my first trip to Australia, I kept tipping out of habit.)

She was absolutely amazed that I was able to compartmentalize what had happened…put the insult in its proper place and not internalize it. She asked me, "How can you be so nonchalant about such blatant insults?" (This was not the first time she had witnessed it – and clearly it wasn't my imagination!)

I suppose the answer is simply that I've lived with it the majority of my life. At some point, you simply have to stop being offended by ignorance, because if you don't, you'll be upset every day. I decided decades ago that I would not give my power to another person.

So should I be forced to change myself (my size, facial features, teeth, education, etc.) to reach my goals...to achieve success?

This goes back to one of the earlier chapters in this book. Regardless if it's career, pageant, or entrepreneurially related, you must know your destination, know where you are headed, and what it is going to take for you to be successful at reaching that destination. You must be realistic about the requirements necessary to reach *your* chosen destination so that *you* are not disappointed.

For example, if your desired destination is to be a doctor, lawyer or congresswoman, then clearly "just being yourself" won't get the job done. Trying to achieve those destinations without the appropriate education is undoubtedly an unrealistic expectation. You can apply or pursue it relentlessly, but the reality of you achieving that destination is slim to "Are you kidding me?"

There are other industries where certain unwritten criteria may exist, but you can work around the criteria. It's long been known that the pharmaceutical industry tends to hire young men and women for sales people who are more, shall we say, pleasing to the eye.

Now, they don't advertise that, and they certainly would never tell you that you aren't being hired to work for them because you don't meet that "criteria." But when is the last time you saw a pharmaceutical rep that was fifty years old, overweight, or who didn't look like Barbie or Ken? Yes, they exist, but how often?

Clearly if you want to get a job as a pharmaceutical sales rep, you would have to be able to offer one of two things in order to be considered...eye-catching looks OR you would have to be such an outstanding sales person that they would be crazy not to hire you even if you don't look like Barbie or Ken.

Often when coaching pageant competitors, I have to address the issue of weight. It's one of the hardest conversations I have to have, but it's usually a very effective one. I will share this message with my clients:

"As a plus-size woman, I am the last person in the world to tell you that you have to lose weight or change your appearance to be successful. That is simply not true! There are countless areas where your size or appearance does not factor into your ability to excel and be great at what you do. BUT…if your desired destination includes winning a pageant, it will be in your best interest to understand that one of the requirements in *this* industry is a healthy, nutritionally sound, height-weight proportioned body. This is most likely non-negotiable if you want to win."

There are just certain industries where carrying weight (or any number of other liabilities) will be a very hard to overcome. Can it be done? Sure! Is it going to be easy? Probably not!

As of the writing of this book, under the laws enforced by the Equal Employment Opportunity Commission, it is illegal to discriminate against someone (applicant or employee) because of that person's race, color, religion, sex (including pregnancy), national origin, age (forty or older), disability or genetic information. It is also illegal to retaliate against a person because he or she complained about discrimination, filed a charge of discrimination, or participated in an employment discrimination investigation or lawsuit. (http://www.eeoc.gov/laws/practices/index.cfm)

So let's see if we have this straight. You can be bat shit crazy, have a genetic predisposition, or be older than dirt, and an employer (or potential employer) cannot use that as a reason not to hire you. Thank goodness!

Just exactly where in that EEOC guideline does it say that hiring someone based on physical appearance is discriminatory? Disability and age – yes! Barbie and Ken...that's another story!

Truth be known, companies still turn people away for the very reasons that the law prohibits. They just disguise it under a plethora of other reasons. The problem is, it's hard to prove that they do it.

So if a company can still figure out how to turn people away for illegal reasons, what makes you think that other *legal* parameters (something that isn't listed as discriminatory) aren't being taken into consideration?

The point to this discussion is simple. If you discover that you may not meet the requirements necessary to reach your life or career destination, you have to decide if you are up for the challenge to prove them wrong. Do you have enough Moxie to break the rules, step outside the box, try something new or different, even if you don't meet the stereotype?

I've had to embrace the fact that if I choose to remain a plus-size woman, I have to be willing to be so outstanding at what I do that people will be willing to overlook it and consider me anyway.

A great example of this phenomenon presents itself in the pageantry world. Since I coach primarily in the rodeo queen world, I'll use that example, but what I'm about to share is true across *all* areas of life.

Since the late 1980s, I have been coaching pageant competitors. Every year I find myself having major debates with some of the girls I'm coaching about what is appropriate in pageant attire.

A few years ago the big debate was over a black hat. Every time I told a young lady that she needed to wear a black hat with her outfit, I got this response...

"You can't wear a black hat!"

"Who told you that?" I asked.

"*They* told me that I have to wear a white hat."

"*They* who?"

"Everyone."

Then I would ask the critical question, "Why?"

"I don't know! They just said you can't wear a black hat."

To quote from today's social media circles…OMG! I heard this feedback from every place I turned *until* Miss Rodeo Utah 2012, Chenae' Shiner submitted her photo for the Miss Rodeo America program book. Her stunning, artistic photo featured Shiner in a black outfit, with a black background and a black hat. But the icing on the cake was when she won the title of Miss Rodeo America 2013. OH NO! Say it isn't so!

I just shook my head and wondered, "What would *they* say about this?"

In this world there are leaders and there are followers. Women with Moxie are leaders. They take calculated risks, step outside the box, and stretch their wings. But they always know one thing for sure…if you step outside the box, you better be so good at what you do that *they* would be crazy to fault you for the risk you took.

Once she won the national title, black hats started popping up everywhere. Even the Miss Rodeo America professional photo shoots featured the national titleholders in black, white, and even tan hats.

Moxie Minute:

If people like you, they may
overlook your shortcomings.
If they don't, they may
use your shortcomings against you!

If you have built rapport with people, won them over, created a bond with them *and* you have shown how talented you are within your field, people are more likely to overlook when you step outside the box, change up the "norm", or take calculated risks.

Another very important characteristic for women with Moxie is knowing when and how to apply the Moxie. There is a time and place for everything, and part of being successful is being able to discern when is the right time and where is the right place to go for it.

Studies have shown that if you make a bad first impression, it can take fifteen to twenty additional positive encounters to change that person's impression of you. It's exhausting just thinking about trying to turn around a bad first impression.

Several years ago I arrived home late Friday night after completing a two-week long stint on the road facilitating seminars. After traveling and training for fourteen years, my friends and family all know not to call me on Saturdays before noon because it's my day to sleep in and catch up on everything I need to do from the week of work.

This particular Saturday I woke up thinking I could hear water running, but decided it was the neighbor running water outside and fell back to sleep. A short time later my dog jumped up on the bed and woke me up with four soaking wet paws. I knew immediately that wet paws at 7:30 in the morning couldn't be good news.

I jumped out of bed to find my bathroom flooded from an overflowing toilet. Water was standing on the floor. I shut off the water to the house first thing, started grabbing towels to mop up the water and then realized that I was going to need a plunger and a wet vac.

A trip to the men's toy store (Home Depot) was now in order and was the last place I wanted to be at 8:30 on a Saturday morning. Every man in a three county radius was at Home Depot to buy all the things they needed to complete this week's "honey-do" lists and special projects. And now I had to tap into my inner "peacock" to mingle with them in the long checkout line.

As I stood there with a plunger in one hand and a wet vac in the other, I suddenly realized that I hadn't cleaned up before heading out of the house. After sleeping all night, my short red hair was standing straight up on my head like a Mohawk. I had pulled on an old pair of sweats and a t-shirt, and I didn't have any make-up on. Well, that is partially true…I didn't have any fresh make-up on. What I had on was left over from the night before, but it now looked like war paint streaked down my face.

The gentleman in front of me turned around and said, "Oh no. That doesn't look good! Toilet overflow?"

"You guessed it," I unenthusiastically replied. "Looks like you're building something," I continued, based on the lumber on his flatbed cart.

After some dialogue back and forth, I asked him "Do you live close by? What do you do?"

"I'm the CEO of XYZ Company."

Nooooooo, not XYZ Company! Anywhere but there! He worked for a company that I had been trying to get into as a third-party training vendor for months. And there he stood looking at me with my Mohawk and plunger in hand. Again, God has a sense of humor!

I prayed that he would not ask me what I do, but to no avail. "What do *you* do?"

I thought for a split second and then replied, "I'm a sales consultant." I didn't tell him I was a corporate trainer.

People will say to me, "Why didn't you just tell him the truth? He would have understood under the circumstances."

No…he wouldn't have. I was a mid-fifties, plus-size woman, with make-up streaking across my face, a flaming red Mohawk, wearing stained sweat pants and a t-shirt, holding a plunger in my hand. This might have been my only chance to make a great first impression and the last thing I wanted to do was tell him that I was the president of Image Development Group.

(Enter sarcasm here:) "Yes sir, I develop images for a living. I train people how to put their best foot forward and how to be successful. What are you thinking about *this* look I'm sporting today?" That was not the impression I wanted to burn into his memory bank. In addition, I wasn't sure if I left him with that first impression, if I would actually have 15-20 additional opportunities to change that picture of me.

In this situation, "just being myself" *may* have cost me a lead. I realize that I've talked earlier in the book about not making assumptions, about getting information and details before assuming things about another person or another situation.

But let's not forget the message of this chapter, "What people see is what they think they are getting." In this situation, there was a "wild card" involved. The wild card was that I had no way of knowing if this gentleman would or would not understand my situation. I had to quickly evaluate if I was willing to take that chance; was I willing to take a calculated risk and possibly make a bad first impression? Would I have the opportunities to overcome a bad first impression if necessary?

In that split second, I felt it was in my best interest to assume he might not understand. That way, I would be more likely to have an opportunity in the future.

This experience taught me that while others may be able to have the weekend off and be scruffy, that was not something that my career was going to afford me. Everyone I happen to run into, no matter where I go, could turn into a potential lead or new client. At the very least, I needed to fix my hair, put on clean clothes and slap on some fresh mascara and lipstick. That is the cost of being a self-employed motivational speaker and corporate trainer.

There is a lot of competition out there...in all areas of life. The bottom line is that every industry has certain requirements that you must meet in order to be successful in that industry.

You absolutely have to decide if you meet the requirements that are necessary in your industry of choice. If not, is it possible for you to make those changes? If yes, do you want to be successful in that industry enough to do whatever it takes to succeed?

If not, that's okay, but don't get upset if you don't reach your goal in that industry.

WOMEN WITH MOXIE:

- Don't internalize comments or take things personally for long.
- Don't let "NO" stop them from pushing forward. They find a way over, under, around or through obstacles.
- Are leaders, not followers! They take calculated risks, step outside the box, and stretch their wings.
- Know when and how to apply the Moxie. There is a time and place for everything, and part of being successful is being able to discern when is the right time and where is the right place to go for it.

YOUR MOXIE MISSION
(Should You Choose to Accept It)

1. It's time to have a self-evaluation. Stand in front of the mirror and be brutally honest with yourself. What do you see in the mirror? Make a list of all the thoughts that come to you. This is NOT a self-disparagement session; it is a self-discovery session. The purpose is for you to acknowledge who you are, what you look like, what are your assets AND your liabilities.
2. Write down your top two or three life or career destinations (goals). Give this some thought. This can be a career goal, a pageant goal, or a goal to start your own business.
3. Make a list of every requirement for this goal(s) you can think of. Education, experience, physical health, appearance, etc. Be honest with yourself. Don't list what you think the requirements *should* be – but what they really are.
4. Compare your self-evaluation list with the goal requirement list you created in step three.
5. Are there any requirements that you currently do not meet or where you are lacking?
6. If yes, is it possible for you to change something to meet the requirement?
    a. If yes, are you willing to commit to making those changes?
    b. If yes, what is it going to take to make those changes?
    DO IT!

c. If no, are you willing to move forward toward that goal knowing that you are going to have to work around that liability? This may require Moxie – fortitude, focus, being better at everything else you can do to overcome your liability.

CHAPTER 9

College and Knowledge Are Not the Same Thing

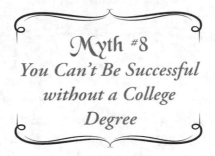

Myth #8
You Can't Be Successful without a College Degree

B eing a corporate trainer for a living, I am a firm believer in education, training, and continued learning. However, being a person who does not have a traditional degree, I may have a different take on education than most.

I represent a very large group of people in the United States who do not have a formal college degree. In fact, according to the United States Census Bureau, as of the end of 2013, the percentage of people ages twenty-five and older who had a bachelor's degree or higher was 28.8%. By the end of 2014, that figure had only increased to 32% (http://quickfacts.census.gov/qfd/states/00000.html).

So even though we are told continuously that in order to be successful, we must have a formal degree, and that a master's degree is the new bachelor's, 68% of the population did not have a bachelor's degree or above at the end of 2014. This brings me to the point of this chapter.

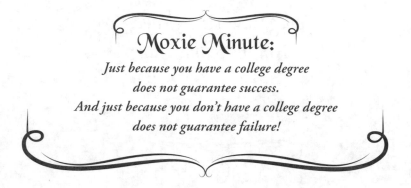

Moxie Minute:

*Just because you have a college degree
does not guarantee success.
And just because you don't have a college degree
does not guarantee failure!*

As I mentioned earlier, my parents talked me out of going to college based on their experiences in life. Remember, they both had eighth-grade educations and my father got his high school GED in order to promote into management in the gas pipeline industry. So when it came time for me to go to college, they did not teach me the importance of a formal education. Instead, they taught me the importance of hard work.

As I entered the traditional job market, however, I soon learned that having a degree could certainly provide an advantage. So in my mid-twenties, while working full-time and getting married, I enrolled at a very well-known community college in the Kansas City area and spent a few years working toward a major in marketing and management with a minor in fashion merchandising. Based on my GPA, I was fortunate enough to receive a full academic scholarship.

After completing fifty-eight credit hours (only nine credit hours short of achieving my associate's degree) I found myself getting a divorce and having to get re-established on my own. Here's your lemon...

I hired an attorney to help me with the strange divorce issues I mentioned earlier. Although he agreed that the situation with my ex-husband and his new wife (with my same name) was unique and that I certainly had a claim, he proceeded to tell me that I didn't have enough money to fight the situation. He advised that I move to another state and start my life over. So I did. I packed up everything I owned and moved to a small community in northeast Missouri where some rodeo friends were living.

This change temporarily brought my college career to a screeching halt. I had to put my education on hold so I could start over, which would end up being the first of several "do-overs" I would experience in my life.

Soon after relocating, I secured a job as the administrative assistant to the assistant academic dean at Northeast Missouri State University (now called Truman State University). Since the biggest challenge I was facing was how to financially survive *and* pay for and attend college, I was very excited about this new job. I would now be entitled to discounts on college tuition, and I was working on campus. Ta-da! Problem solved!

I met with the lady to talk about getting my credit hours transferred and to organize my plan of action. I proudly handed her my transcripts boasting the 4.0 GPA I had acquired in marketing and management. After five short minutes, she advised me that only twelve of the fifty-eight credit hours were going to transfer. What?

Then she informed me that while I could enroll in courses, I would not be able to claim a major because I had never taken the college entrance exams. As you will recall, my parents encouraged me to get a job in my senior year of high school and I had not taken college prep classes since I wouldn't be going to college. As a result, I had never taken algebra, geometry, or science, and I was pretty certain I would not be able to pass the college entrance exams.

But when you are a woman with Moxie, you find a way over, under, around, or through all obstacles in order to reach your desired goal. I made a suggestion that caught the woman off guard. I asked her if I could simply take the courses that were required for my major, including the courses I would need in order to pass the entrance exams, and then in my final year take those exams and claim my major.

She looked at me and replied, "In twenty-five years of working here, no one has ever asked me that. I don't know the answer. Let me find out." Turns out I could have done just that! The only possible glitch would be that my major requirements might change before I finished.

Our society is told repetitively that having a college degree opens the doors to more opportunities and/or higher paying careers. And I don't necessarily disagree. College is a wonderful institution. There is no doubt that education is a minimum and mandatory requirement if you want to be successful. But let's get one thing straight:

College and knowledge are NOT the same thing!

I walked away from the entire college experience feeling like it really wasn't about me getting an education. I didn't feel like anyone was really in my corner, wanting to help me get "educated". It just seemed based on all of my college experiences that it was about jumping through hoops, attending the *right* college, and the social experience.

Yes…I understand that my situation may have been unique because I didn't attend college right out of high school. Had I been properly prepped for college it probably would have been a smoother process and I would have completed my formal education.

My experience however, might be one explanation for the extremely low bachelor's or above completion rate. If it's this difficult to go back to college if you don't go straight out of high school, no wonder people don't go back.

Where does that leave the almost 70% of the population, like myself, who don't have a formal degree? Are we to believe that our career options are minimal? The answer is NO!

Before I dive into this topic, let me say that I am approaching this from a logical and ROI (Return on Investment) standpoint. Hands down, education and knowledge are critical to success. But speaking from personal experience, I can assure you that you *can* obtain an education, be knowledgeable, and be successful without a formal degree.

After teaching this information in a seminar, a young woman approached me and said, "I called my mom at lunch and told her that I was ready to drop out of college. After hearing everything you shared, I'm thinking it might be a waste of my time."

I looked at her and said, "I'll tell you why you don't want to quit college. If you haven't majored in MOXIE, you may not have the guts and gumption necessary to be successful without a degree to open doors for you. I would strongly recommend that you continue your education, but start learning about creating multiple streams of income and passive income too."

Clearly having a college degree can open doors for you. If you don't have a degree, you may have to kick doors down. That is where Moxie comes into play! The problem is that people may not be willing to put in the time and effort, or may not have the Moxie necessary to kick down doors.

The first time I read that almost 70% of our population did not have a bachelor's degree or higher, I was shocked. I was absolutely sure that with all the hype about college, that percentage would have been lower.

Then I started thinking, if getting a degree is instrumental in getting a better or higher paying job, what in the world are those non-degreed people doing? So I did some research.

- Bill Gates, the world's richest man, dropped out of Harvard and co-founded Microsoft and is estimated to be worth $76 billion.
- The flamboyant performer Lady Gaga ditched college and has sold 27 million albums globally.
- Television host, commentator, and author Sean Hannity worked his way from a local radio show to hosting very popular news and talk radio shows.
- Founder of Whole Foods, John Mackey, today has a grocery chain of 387 stores and $10 billion in revenue.
- Where would Dell computers be today without Michael Dell, who by age twenty-seven was the CEO of the Fortune 500 Company and is worth $18.7 billion.
- Probably one of the greatest golfers of all time, Tiger Woods left Stanford and has won fourteen major championships (not to mention securing endorsements).
- Sean Combs (P Diddy) released twenty-seven different platinum albums, launched a clothing line, and has a net worth estimated at $700 million.
- Mark Zuckerberg, CEO and founder of Facebook, has over a billion users around the world and an estimated net worth of $13.3 billion.
- Conservative radio talk show host Rush Limbaugh is estimated to have earned over $66 million dollars.
- The world's favorite self-centered performer Kanye West has become one of the wealthiest men in America.
- Sheldon Adelson, CEO of the Las Vegas Sands, has been credited with creating over fifty businesses in his career.
- Founder of Napster, Sean Parker, today claims a net worth estimated over $2 billion.
- Music mogul and founder of Dreamworks and Geffen Records, David Geffen, has a net worth of $6 billion.

- And last but not least, Steve Jobs, co-founder of Apple, reported an estimated net worth of $8.3 billion.
  - http://dailycaller.com/2014/09/25/the-daily-caller-presents-the-top-16-successful-people-who-dont-have-college-degrees/
  - http://www.cheatsheet.com/hot-feature/8-billionaires-who-never-bothered-to-get-a-college-degree.html/?a=viewall

Love them, or hate them, you can't deny their success. So if they don't have a degree and they have experienced this kind of success, what did they have? Moxie! Guts, gumption, fortitude, focus, commitment, and hard work. They didn't take "no" for an answer.

In fact, if you do a little research on Google you can find thousands of people who are famous, rich, and/or successful who are also high school or college dropouts.

Everywhere we turn, we are told that going to college provides better career opportunities and/or better paying jobs. Unfortunately, the studies, reports, and surveys don't always support that statement.

According to the National Association of College and Employers' (NACE) April 2014 Salary Survey, the overall average starting salary for a 2013 college graduate was $45,473.

- www.naceweb.org/uploadedFiles/Content/static-assets/downloads/executive-summary/2014-april-salary-survey-executive-summary.pdf

On the flip side of the coin, according to a September 23, 2014 article posted on the Market Watch website entitled, "The 10 Best-Paying Jobs that Don't Require a College Degree", the annual median salary ranged from $63,680 to $83,890.

- http://www.marketwatch.com/story/10-best-paying-jobs-for-high-school-grads-2014-09-23

Here's an interesting statistic that was featured in a January 30, 2015 article entitled, "How Much Does it Cost to Study in the US", published by QS Top Universities Worldwide University Rankings, Guides and Events:

> *In HSBC's 2014 report on the costs of studying abroad in different locations, the US emerged as the third most-expensive option overall, behind Australia and Singapore. HSBC put the average annual cost of study in the US – including tuition fees and living expenses – at $36,564. Multiply that by four years for most undergraduate courses and by six years for most master's degrees, and for the majority of prospective students, attending a university in the US may seem about as realistic as crashing at the White House while you look for a place to live.*
>
> *When transport and other living expenses are factored in, College Board estimates the following annual budgets for undergraduate students in 2014/15:*
>
> - *$16,325 (community college)*
> - *$23,410 (in-state students at a four-year public college)*
> - *$37,229 (out-of-state students at a four-year public college)*
> - *$46,272 (private non-profit four-year college)*
>
> *Admittedly, you can't complete a full degree at a two-year college, but you can gain an associate's degree. This counts as the first half of a bachelor's degree, which can then be completed by transferring to a university for an additional two or three years.*

I love that last statement. Maybe it has changed today. Maybe today all the credits you earn with an associate's degree do transfer. But that wasn't my experience. And even if they do transfer today, my guess is it takes advanced planning and coordinating with both colleges to make sure their programs transfer seamlessly.

Do these reports and statistics mean that we're being sold a false bill of goods about the importance of a college degree? Absolutely not! There is no doubt that having a college degree can open career doors. Many of the highest paying jobs in the US today are as a result of having advanced degrees. Let's face it; I would not want someone operating on me, or representing me in a courtroom, who had not received a formal education and degree in their field.

When you weigh out the benefits of *having* a degree against the cost of *getting* a degree, I believe it becomes necessary to really step back and evaluate your goals, your desired destination, the requirements, and yourself. Are you seeking a career that *requires* a degree (doctor, lawyer, engineer, etc.)? If your answer is yes, then obtaining an advanced college degree is a non-negotiable course of action.

If your desired destination does not require a formal degree, then you have to ask yourself if you are prepared to kick down doors to reach your goals? Are you ready to go over, under, around, and through any obstacle to get where you want to be? Do you have Moxie?

If you are attending college because your career destination requires it, or you personally want or need social/personal growth (which going to college does provide), or you want a degree in your back pocket in case you need it —- great!

Just to be clear, I did *not* share this information as proof that you *don't* need or *shouldn't* attend college. My point is that if you don't have a degree, you are in good company. "Just because you don't have a degree does not guarantee failure."

The remainder of this chapter is directed to people who think they can't be successful because they don't have that formal college degree. The truth is you CAN be successful. It just takes opening up you mind and kicking your MOXIE into high gear. Those of you who do have a college degree might want to read this as well!

I am a firm believer that at some point, you may want to step back and look at education more from a "return on investment" (ROI) standpoint.

If you are going to college because everyone tells you that you should, that might not be the right reason. For example, whenever

I talk about not having a degree, people immediately say to me, "It's not too late. You can still get your degree. You should do that!" Yes, I could. But then my logic kicks in. I'm in my mid-fifties. The fifty-eight credit hours that I earned back in the 1980s didn't transfer in the 1980s – why would they have any value today? This means I would most likely have to start completely over and go through at least four years of schooling just to get a bachelor's degree. I would have to continue working to support myself, so I would have to take classes part-time, which would turn a four-year degree into a five or six-year degree. I would incur possible school loans (debt), which would have to be repaid. All so I could do what I love to do — speaking, training, and motivating! WAIT... I'm already doing that, debt free. Now tell me again why I would want/ need to get a degree?

There isn't a financial planner in the world who would call that a good return on your investment of time and money.

So let's get down to the nitty-gritty of this chapter.

- Do you need a formal college degree to be successful? No!
- Can a formal college degree be beneficial in opening doors for your future? Yes!
- Can you be successful and earn a solid living without a college degree? Yes!
  (But…it depends on what your career interests are. What is your desired career "destination"? This goes back to a former chapter where we talked about how "destinations" have certain requirements in order to even think about them.)
- Does having a degree create financial security? NO! Absolutely not! College and wealth are not the same thing either!

Regardless if you have a degree or not, creating financial security is based on an entirely different set of standards. I can't begin to tell you how many people I know with advanced degrees who are broke, financially dependent on a J.O.B. (Just Over Broke), and have no freedom. That is working hard, not smart. College and knowledge are not the same thing.

I commented earlier in the book that whenever I talk about money, making money, or being financially secure, people will often quip back to me, "Money doesn't buy happiness," or "Money ain't everything!" Well...true. Money ain't everything. But it's right up there with air. You cannot survive without it.

I agree that money doesn't buy happiness, but what I *do* know is that it takes money today to build churches, to fund missions, to donate to charities, or to put your children through college. I also believe that money only makes you more of what you already are. If you are a selfish person, money will only make you more selfish. If you are a giving person, you will use money to help others.

I'm not talking about being stinkin' filthy rich here. I'm talking about being stinkin' filthy secure or independent – not having to rely on a J.O.B. to survive. The truth of the matter is, having a college degree is not required to achieve financial independence.

Ask any financial planner, or economic strategist, and they will tell you that the key to financial security is passive income and/or multiple streams of income. Guess what? This requires knowledge and hard work.

Through research, it has been determined that most millionaires today have at least seven different sources of income. They not only understand the power of multiple streams of income and passive income, but they implement that theory on a regular basis.

As defined by Wikipedia, passive income is:

An income received on a regular basis, with little effort required to maintain it. It is closely related to the concept of "unearned income".

The American Internal Revenue Service categorizes income into three broad types, active (earned) income, passive (unearned) income, and portfolio income. It defines passive income as only coming from two sources: rental activity or "trade or business activities in which you do not materially participate." Other financial and government institutions also recognize it as an income obtained as a result of capital growth or in relation to negative gearing. Passive income is usually taxable.

SOME EXAMPLES OF PASSIVE INCOME ARE.

- *Any type of property income*
- *Earnings from a business that does not require direct involvement from the owner or merchant*
- *Rent from property*
- *Interest from a bank account*
- *Royalties from publishing a book or from licensing a patent or other form of intellectual property, such as computer software products*
- *Earnings from internet advertisements on websites*
- *Dividend and interest income from owning securities, such as stocks and bonds, is usually referred to as portfolio income, which may or may not be considered a form of passive income. In the United States, portfolio income is considered a different type of income than passive income*
- *Pensions.*

The way I explain passive income is a little less formal – "Something that allows you to earn money while you are off doing something else" – like sitting on the beach, or traveling, or spending time with your grandchildren.

When you look at all of those non-degreed people I listed earlier, who are more than financially secure, I believe you will notice a pattern. Most of them are involved in some form of passive income (royalties, investments, real estate, etc.).

People will often say to me, "I started my own business making jewelry (or some other endeavor). Isn't that a good thing?"

Yes! Having a home business is definitely a good thing, *as long as* you are treating it like a business. Setting up an office or work area in your home (regardless if it is part-time or full-time) allows you to take advantage of tax deductions on your income tax.

In my case, because I am self-employed full-time and travel for a living, my car is titled to my corporation so I pay for the car payments, taxes, insurance, and maintenance from the business and then I am able to write those expenses off as business expenses.

Unfortunately, making jewelry in your home to sell (or any home business where you are the only person creating the product or providing the service) would not be considered passive income. The reason is that if something happened to you, and you had to stop creating your product or providing your service, your income would likewise stop.

On the other hand, if you are involved in a business where you invest the majority of your time upfront building the business and then you continue to earn money when you step away, that is passive income.

Examples of businesses that provide passive income would be a car wash (where people drop quarters and wash their own car), a pay laundry, creating an online store where people can buy online and you drop ship (not design but buy and re-sell), create webinars and sell registrations to attend. The list goes on and on.

Setting up investment programs (401K, annuities, stocks, bonds, etc.) is another common way to create passive income. You invest money in one of the many options out there, and you earn interest on that money while you are off going to work every day. The mistake most people make here is waiting too late to set up accounts and start depositing money. Even if you can only deposit $20 a month, DO IT! Set up accounts and start building!

One of the most talked about methods of creating passive income is real estate…rental property, commercial property, and/or flipping properties for a profit. With rental properties, you buy a property and then rent it to cover your mortgage payment, insurance, taxes, and maintenance. This allows you to build equity in property while someone else (the renter) is paying the bills. In addition, you can deduct all the expenses of the property off your taxes as a business expense.

Now, let's be honest here. All real estate investment is work, and you do have to stay on top of things, but you aren't tethered by a ball and chain once you get the properties going and rented. What it does take is due diligence (research) and knowledge – not college.

I'm sure you realize that most of these passive income ideas require upfront investment. You have to buy real estate in order to rent it. You have to buy or build a car wash in order to run it. You get the point here. So what do you do when you don't have a ton of money to invest upfront?

Another widely popular passive income source for people wanting to start a business with limited funds to invest is network marketing (aka multi-level marketing, direct sales). NO not a pyramid scheme…network marketing. There is a difference! Pyramid schemes are illegal. Network marketing is a viable business ownership option. Let me assure you, if network marketing wasn't legitimate, the Federal Trade Commission would have them shut down immediately.

Quite often when I offer this as an option for people, they will immediately say, "No, I'm not interested in that pyramid stuff." That usually tells me they have not done their own research about the industry or company instead of listening to half-truths from others, or they don't have enough Moxie to do whatever it takes to be financially independent. They have most likely listened to someone who really has no idea what the difference is, or they know someone "who got involved in that scheme and didn't make any money."

Well, that can be a true statement for every single option I've mentioned here. Whether you buy a car wash, open a coin laundry, or buy jewelry and sell it through an online "store", YOU have to be committed to getting the business off the ground, stay consistent, stay focused on your long-term goals, and actually "show up to work" every day. Bottom line...if YOU don't work the business, the business doesn't work! This takes Moxie!

Speaking from personal experience, I would strongly recommend that you keep your options open when it comes to this type of business. For those of you who haven't done your research, let me offer this information.

According to the Federal Trade Commission, some people confuse pyramid and Ponzi schemes with legitimate network marketing opportunities. Network marketing programs, unlike pyramid or Ponzi schemes, have a real product to sell. More importantly, they actually sell product to members of the general public, without *requiring* these consumers to pay anything extra or to join the network. While they may pay commissions to a long string of distributors, these commissions are paid for real retail sales, not for new recruits.

In a pyramid scheme, an organization compels individuals to make a payment strictly for joining the organization. In exchange, the organization promises its new members a share of the money taken from every additional member that they recruit. The directors of the organization (those at the top of the pyramid) also receive a share of these payments.

Such organizations seldom involve sales of products or services with real value. Without creating any goods or services, the only ways for a pyramid scheme to generate revenue are to recruit more members or solicit more money from current members.

I have personally always had my hand in network marketing because it was a great way to build income that didn't require 100% of my time. But I'm not alone it seems.

In an article in the *Pittsburgh Courier* (March 6, 2014) entitled "Successful Women Make Their Mark in Network Marketing".

I see tremendous value in network marketing and understand why so many women are getting involved,' said Donna M. Baxter, president of NAWBO (National Association of Women Business Owners) Greater Pittsburgh. She pointed out that statistics indicate that 82% of women in the United States who make $100,000 a year or more accomplished it through direct sales.

There are even some universities today that are offering classes and certificates in network marketing. In an article on MLMAttorney.com, entitled, "Why Don't Business Schools Teach Network Marketing in Their Curricula?" we read:

Some colleges have noticed that network marketing is underrepresented in business schools and have been offering classes and certificates in network marketing. Bethany College, for example, offers a network marketing certificate, as well as a marketing major with a network marketing emphasis. The college reports that it seeks to promote integrity, trust and transparency in network marketing.

Even earlier, Utah Valley State offered a course on network marketing using the book, Network Marketing: What You Should Know by Jeffrey Babener as course material. Seminars in network marketing have been presented at University of Illinois at Chicago, University of Texas at El Paso and University of Houston. Case studies of direct selling companies have been utilized at the college and graduate level and numerous academic studies have been published pursuant to grants from the Direct Selling Education Foundation (DSEF).

While some colleges may offer courses in network marketing, you do NOT need a college degree to be successful at network marketing. What you need is Moxie, a can-do attitude, an affiliation with a great company and product, and a commitment to reach your goal.

I will caution you, however, that network marketing companies are not created equal. I was involved with a skin care company for over fifteen years and because of their very restricting "independent contractor" agreement, I was constantly being threatened with deregistration because I was supposedly using my affiliations within that company to promote my speaking career or other companies. In fact, this company even thought they had the right to dictate to me how and where I could promote this book once it was released. That is not the definition of an "independent contractor". Know the law!

I can assure you there are several *really* great legitimate network marketing companies out there that do get it, and that allow you to promote your business and products using social media platforms. In fact, the company I'm affiliated with today has over 161 associates who are now earning seven figures a year, and countless others who are earning solid six-figure incomes.

Experts say you should pick a company that has been in business for at least five years, and that markets a consumable product (a product that you use, use up and have to replace – this creates repeat orders). In addition, you should be prepared to make at least a three-year commitment to a company before deciding it doesn't work. It's no different than any other business you would start. It takes time to build it, find clients, and train team members. How fast it grows is *completely* based on your level of commitment.

Just make sure you read the policies before you get involved to make sure it works with your lifestyle and other business ventures.

At the end of the day, this all means that in order to be successful, you need an education — knowledge. Whether you get that knowledge in college, seminars, industry conferences, or through your own self-commitment to continued learning is up to you! If you want to obtain a college degree, I say **go for it**! In our society it will certainly help open doors for you in your career.

But if your goal is to have financial security or to be financially independent, you will need much more than a college degree. You will want to learn about and invest time creating passive and/or multiple streams of income *in addition* to your advanced degrees.

WOMEN WITH MOXIE:

- Understand the need for and value of education. They take advantage of all learning opportunities presented to them.
- Don't allow the lack of a degree to stop them. They invest in and gain knowledge from other sources (books, audios, videos, seminars, etc.) and invest their time where they can get the most "bang for their buck!"
- Never take "no" for an answer without asking questions, researching, or finding out if there is another way. They are out of the box thinkers.
- Understand the power of creating multiple streams of income (income from more than one source). They never put all their eggs in one basket.

YOUR MOXIE MISSION
(Should You Choose to Accept It)

1. Have you achieved your career/life destinations/goals?
   a. If yes – congratulations.
   b. If no – what is stopping you from reaching those goals?
      i. If a formal degree is required to reach your career destination, then make that happen!
      ii. If a formal degree is not required, then start making a list of exactly what you need to do to achieve your goals. Then figure out how to go over, under, around, or through obstacles to achieve that.
2. Do you currently have a bachelor's degree or above?
   a. If yes – do you regularly invest in continued learning of some kind? Do you have your own educational library? If not, start adding resources to your own knowledge library.
   b. If no – see #3 below!
3. Has "life" gotten in the way of you finishing your college education? Would scholarships help you to get back on track? Check out this awesome application that will give you access to well over 10,000 potential scholarships in seconds. It's only .99 to download. Go to: https://www.myscholly.com.
4. Are you financially secure? (If you lost your J.O.B. today, could you live without it?) If you are not financially secure, it's time, right now, to do something to change that. YOU are the only person who can do it.

a. Figure out which form of passive income you would like to start learning about (investments, real estate, network marketing, online sales, or webinars, etc.)

b. If you choose investments, meet with a Financial Planner to teach you about your options and what you need to do to get started. And remember, even if you only have $20 a month to invest today, DO IT! Don't let anyone tell you otherwise!

c. If you choose real estate, start doing research or call people in those industries to pick their brain. Be very, very careful about spending money to attend seminars where they are trying to sell you on a real estate program. With some committed research and due diligence, you can learn what you need to know for free, or at the very least for the cost of a few books or lunches (buying lunch for someone who is providing you with information)

d. If you are going to check into a network marketing organization, again do your research.

e. Google and read everything you can on the area(s) you choose

CHAPTER 10

Life Is Like An Elevator

Throughout this book, we have discussed eight myths, lies or half-truths that seem to prevent women from being strong or having enough Moxie to be successful.

In this chapter, we will focus on a very valuable truth that you must keep in mind as you take your life journey. No matter what *your* definition of success is, what your life/career destination is, how many lemons life has handed you, or what your personal challenges are, everyone has experienced the many ways that life is like an elevator.

For example:

- The sole purpose of an elevator is to help people reach their destination.
- Elevators go up and down.
- There are times when you will get off on the wrong floor and have to get back on and start over to reach your destination.
- People riding elevators may or may not like you, may or may not support you, may or may not care about you.
- As elevators go up and down, they stop to allow people to get on and off.
- There's always someone who will get on an elevator and push all the buttons.
- Often, by the time an elevator reaches the top floor, you may be the only person left on the elevator.

Let's explore how these truths may affect your life and/or career journey.

LIFE PURPOSE

Just like an elevator, your life and/or career should have a purpose…a destination. I think we can all agree that if you work in an elevator rich environment, during the course of a day, your destinations can change or be detoured when you least expect it. We talked about this in chapter five, "The Road to Success is an Eight-Lane Highway Under Construction." Over the course of your life, you may have different destinations that you explore before you settle on your true life or career destination.

According to a study commissioned by DeVry University's Career Advisory Board (conducted by Harris Interactive), the reality is that the average person in today's marketplace could easily end up working twelve to fifteen jobs over the course of their career.

While we often criticize the Millennials for being company hoppers or not being committed to their jobs, they really are not that different than their Baby Boomer predecessors. In my Boomer generation, we were told that we would change careers an average of seven times. That's *careers,* not jobs.

If you get on an elevator and you have no idea which floor you are trying to reach (what your destination is), you might be riding up and down for a while. Life is the same way. You have to know your destination(s) at any given time in order to consistently be moving forward.

THE UPS AND DOWNS

Like an elevator, life has its ups and downs. Everyone has good days and bad days. Everyone has days when they feel like they take two steps forward and one step back.

There is no doubt that life is so much better when the ups happen. Getting a promotion or raise, meeting a new significant other, having a new baby, new grandchildren, or getting a new job can be exciting and uplifting in your life. But what happens when life hits the "ground floor" button on your life elevator?

The difference between someone who reaches their destination and someone who does not may lie in how they handle it or how they react when the downs in life happen. We talked about this in chapter six, "Here's Your Lemon!"

There may be times however, when it makes more sense to go down or step back in order to go up or move forward more effectively.

Over fifteen years of intense travel, I've been on more than my fair share of elevators in hotels and convention centers. I can't begin to tell you how many times I've found myself standing and waiting for an "up" elevator, and when the doors open I find that the car is full. So I have to wait for another elevator.

After this happens two or three times, I begin to realize that even though I'm trying to go "up", when a "down" elevator opens and it's empty, I take the calculated risk that I'll reach my destination faster if I get on it and ride it down until I can press the button to go up again.

I think this often happens in life as well. Have you ever found yourself in a job where you are stuck, stagnant, being held back, or not moving forward at the rate you had hoped? Sometimes a woman with Moxie has to evaluate the situation, determine what is holding her back and then take a calculated risk to take a step backward in order to create a detour that, in the long run, helps her reach her true destination faster.

This might mean making a lateral move within your company, moving to another company but taking a lesser salary to gain more advancement options, or changing careers altogether.

Even in the pageant industry, a girl may be better off taking a year off to grow, mature, and focus on improving her skills, so she is better equipped to reach her goals in the next pageant she competes in.

DUST YOURSELF OFF AND START OVER

We've all done it! You're standing on the elevator, waiting to reach your destination. You're probably engaged in checking emails and text messages so when the elevator doors open you assume it's your floor and step off. The doors shut behind you and you look up only to discover that you have gotten off the elevator too soon. Now, you have to start the process all over again. Push the button and wait!

In chapter six, "Here's Your Lemon!" we discussed the importance of finding the sweetness in situations, and being able to dilute or water down the drama in your life. I have witnessed so many people who get off on the wrong floor and then stand there griping and complaining. I call it "harrumphing". Even though they made the mistake, they are upset and will try to blame anyone and everyone except themselves.

I can't tell you how many times I've stepped off the elevator on the wrong floor. But instead of getting upset about it, I start looking for sugar and water! I check out my surroundings or strike up conversations with the other people while I'm waiting. You just never know what you might learn or find because you stepped off on the wrong floor...information that could possibly help you in the future.

Life is the same way. In chapter five, "The Road To Success is an Eight-Lane Highway Under Construction," we learned that in life you will be faced with roadblocks. You will experience losses, disappointments, and detours. You will take wrong turns, make bad decisions, and suffer the embarrassment of making mistakes publicly.

But you WILL survive! The most important thing to remember is to get up, dust yourself off, push the button on your life elevator to start over and wait patiently for new doors to open. While you're waiting, take in the scenery, figure out the lesson you are supposed to learn, find people who can get you to your destination, and re-group.

Then when the new doors of opportunity open, you'll be ready to go through them stronger, wiser, and more prepared than ever before.

PEOPLE GET ON AND PEOPLE GET OFF

When you get on a crowded elevator on the ground floor and you are making your way to the top floor, the elevator often has to make several stops to let people off at their destination.

During your life or career journey, different people will likewise cross your path. Some come in and out of your life quickly, merely passing you on your journey; some come into your life and stay for a few moments, some stay for the duration. There are times, however, when we invite people who should be in our lives for a moment, to stay much longer than they should: friends, co-workers, or significant others. Sometimes we have a hard time setting boundaries or knowing when to step back from people. We don't want to hurt their feelings, but we are allowing them to negatively impact us instead.

I have been guilty in numerous situations of trying to "drag dead horses across the finish line." This can happen when I'm mentoring in the workplace or coaching young women for pageants. I'll see so much potential in my "student" (often I may see more in them than they see in themselves), and I will begin to metaphorically beg them to be successful. Unfortunately if people don't want something bad enough to do whatever it takes to achieve it, you simply cannot do it for them.

They have to come to the table, engage in the learning process, be willing to make changes, and be open to feedback. In many cases, if you are more committed than the protégé, you end up in a conflict with the person (guilty as charged!).

Always remember that the people you mentor or coach have to invest in themselves before you do. They have to prove to you that they are worth investing in. They should be calling you, excited to share successes and eager to hear critique and feedback for improvement. Quite often I will say the following Moxie Minute to people I am working with:

Moxie Minute:

If you don't think you're worth investing in, why should I invest in you?

Another example of keeping people in your life too long has to do with influence. When I was young, my parents gave me the same message I'm sure most of us have received at one time or another growing up. "We just don't like that little Suzie you're hanging out with." I didn't understand what the issue was and I simply thought my parents were trying to take away my friends. If you're a parent, you know exactly what this means.

Chances are you may have said this to your children as well. Parents don't want their children negatively influenced by other children who are out of control. Guilty by association is only one part of the concern. The real issue is "influenced by association."

I have a really important question for you. When was the last time you looked in the mirror as an adult and said, "I'm not sure I like that Bob or Susan you're hanging out with" to yourself?

Years ago I mentored a young woman who was starting her own business. She worked a regular job as an administrative assistant at a law firm, and worked on her own business part-time on the side. Each week we would talk about her goals and how she was coming along on her journey to her destination. We would set goals for the week and she would start the week like gangbusters. By the next time we would meet she would always comment about how discouraged she was and how she wasn't having any success in promoting her business.

I suggested numerous strategies for her to focus on and implement, but nothing seemed to work. She would always be discouraged and even disappointed with herself when we would meet again.

One day I asked her to take me through her day from waking up to going to bed. As she walked me through her day, she said, "...and then I go to lunch with Margie." "Who is Margie?" I asked. She stopped for a moment and responded, "Margie is another woman who works at the law firm."

"How often do you go to lunch with her?"

Without missing a beat she replied, "Every day!"

I realized I might be on to some new information, so I dug deeper. "Tell me about Margie."

She thought for a moment and then said, "Margie has worked at the law firm for fifteen years. She is a single mother with two children." Then she paused for a moment and announced, "Margie is so negative. In fact, she may be one of the most negative people I know."

And there it was. The culprit…the influencer who was holding her back. She would spend hours a day, including the one free hour she had each day, with this "negaholic" and it was affecting her own mindset, motivation, and focus. Margie had become a major detour on her destination.

How many days do you go to lunch or take breaks with someone in your office who may not be the best influence for you in your career? How many times do you connect with another mother who may not be the best influence on you as you raise your child? The people you spend the most time with actually influence you in these areas of your life.

Moxie Minute:
*We are the average sum of the five people we hang out with the most…
financially, spiritually, physically,
professionally, recreationally.*

Okay, be honest! Did you just do a mental inventory of your friends? Did you cringe, or did you let out a sigh of relief?

Now before you freak out and start terminating friendships, let's evaluate what this really means. I'm not suggesting you need to literally "unfriend" people in your work or life. What I'm suggesting is you need to be clear about your destination and make sure the people you spend the *majority* of your time with are teaching you, supporting you, or helping you to reach that destination (personal, pageant, career, etc.).

When I used to teach seminars on how to become financially independent (not reliant on a J.O.B. – Just Over Broke). I would always tell my audience:

"If you want to be financially independent, stop hanging out with poor people!"

"Of course," people would say as they laughed, because they thought I was being funny. However, this statement is a classic "I could have had a V-8" moment. I'm not just referring to being financially poor. I mean don't hang around people who have a poor spirit (victim mentality), poor attitude (stinkin' thinkin'), poor commitment levels, poor emotional intelligence (can't communicate respectfully through conflict) and of course, who are poor financially.

How can someone who is poor in these areas influence *you* to be rich in these areas?

Elevators are usually very small, limiting the number of people who can travel from floor to floor. In life, you must also have a small inner circle of influence.

Considering that you are the average sum of the five people you hang out with the most, wouldn't it make sense to give some thought to who you surround yourself with on your life or career journey?

Who are the people who can influence you, teach you, help you, promote you, and support you? At some point, you will need to decide who your close influencers are, versus the people who are in your life more generally. These people become part of your valuable inner circle. These are the "five (or more) people you surround yourself with" who can raise your personal average intellectually, mentally, spiritually, physically, and/or financially.

Moxie Minute:

*"Deliberately seek the company of people
who influence you to
think and act on building the life you desire."*
Napoleon Hill
Author – *Think and Grow Rich*

PEOPLE MAY NOT LIKE YOU – SUCK IT UP, BUTTERCUP

In a recent seminar, I had a participant pose a question. "You shared earlier that in order to get ahead in your career you need to be able to win the 'Personality Award.' But what happens when, as a woman, you start to advance in your career and you are alienated by former friends and co-workers?"

I thought for a moment and replied, "Not everybody likes you or likes you being successful! Suck it up, buttercup!"

The unfortunate truth is that insecure people often become jealous when a friend achieves career advancement, finds love, or experiences some other kind of personal success. This is the very reason why you may have to exclude people from your life or career journey. When people become jealous, they often become hateful as well. These people are not the influencers you want in your inner circle.

Another sad truth is that no matter how great you are at something, your efforts may not be appreciated for the same reason. When superiors or co-workers are jealous or intimidated by your talents they may not reward or recognize you like they should. This is another reason why you need that core inner circle of influencers who can provide the recognition and acknowledgment that we all need to keep going on our journey.

The challenge is learning that you cannot internalize or own the insecurities of others when they are misplaced or aimed at you. It can be very difficult to stay confident and avoid self-doubt when you are being criticized, mentally attacked, or not recognized for your achievements.

At the end of the day, keep this thought in mind. Just because someone doesn't seem to like you, doesn't mean they really hate you. Try to support them anyway. Thank them when they provide assistance. Don't be the attitude problem in the relationship. Let them have that one. It takes a confident woman with Moxie to have disagreements with people and still be able to work with them, be on projects or teams with them, or help them.

Moxie Minute:

*Invest your time where you are appreciated,
not where you are tolerated!*

THE BUTTON PUSHERS

It never fails. You're waiting to get on the elevator, trying to reach your floor quickly because you are late for a meeting. The doors open, the elevator is empty, and you take a sigh of relief knowing that you won't have any delays. As you step on and turn to push the button to your floor, you see that someone has pushed all the buttons before stepping off.

Do you have button pushers in your life? Do you have people who just love to stir things up in the workplace or in your life? People who spread rumors, or who always seem to have something negative to say about something or someone? People who just know how to push *your* buttons!

These people create delays in reaching your destination. They plant seeds of self-doubt and can actually cause dissention between you and valuable people in your life.

In order to deal with the button pushers, it will be imperative that you commit to learning and understanding Emotional Intelligence (EI). This is the ability to control your emotional responses when people hit your hot buttons.

There are five key parts to EI, as follows:

1. Self-Awareness: your ability to recognize your own hot buttons or triggers, and understanding why you have them or where they came from. What is it that other people say or do that causes you to have a knee-jerk reaction and why? It's very difficult to do the second part of EI if you haven't acknowledged the first one.

2. Self-Management: I call this pulling the rein in on a run-away emotion. Growing up as an equestrian, I've been on a run-away horse before. One of the ways we attempt to stop it is to grab one rein and slowly begin to pull the horse's head around. This causes the horse to have to circle, and as the circle gets smaller, the horse must slow down. In the same fashion, when something happens that triggers your hot buttons, you have to immediately and metaphorically grab that rein on your emotion and pull it in until you have it under control.

3. Social Awareness: being aware of how your actions and behaviors affect the people around you. I truly believe that today our society has an epidemic of a lack of social awareness. People either walk around with blinders on and can't see how they are affecting others, or quite frankly, they don't care. Social awareness is also known as social skill… the ability to move people in the desired direction.

4. Relationship Management: this is considering other people's feelings, especially when making decisions. Being able to mend fences.

5. Motivation: being driven to achieve for the sake of achievement (not solely based on a reward or carrot).

All of these key EI elements factor in when people start pushing your hot buttons. If we are honest with ourselves, most of the time when people push our buttons, they don't even know they are doing it. Other people may not realize they have affected you the way they did, either because you've never told them in a discussion, or they don't know you well enough to know.

So when someone pushes your buttons, self-awareness kicks in so you can say, "Okay self, this is a hot button…red alert." Then self-management reaches down and grabs the rein on that emotional response that is welling up inside you and begins to pull the rein in to bring it under control.

This gives social awareness time to think through how you want to respond so you can make your point or set your boundary assertively without offending, stepping on toes, or attacking. And through these efforts you stand a better chance of getting the other person to move in the desired direction.

Just for the record, experts tell us that having a high EQ (Emotional Intelligence Quotient) will take you farther in your career and/or other endeavors than having a high IQ (Intelligence Quotient). In layman's terms, being able to control your emotions will take you farther than being smart! Don't ever forget this.

IT'S LONELY AT THE TOP

We've all heard the old saying, "It's lonely at the top." Early in my career, I truly believed that meant being heartless and bulldozing over everyone on your way up the proverbial ladder. I assumed, as a result of this belief, it was lonely at the top because people had abused everyone trying to get to the top.

Having been raised as "the only son my father never had", I was raised to be strong, work hard, not make excuses, and be self-sufficient. What I didn't understand at the time is that I was being groomed to be a business *owner* and entrepreneur, not a corporate ladder climber.

I learned very quickly that sometimes it's lonely at the top because you've had to stand up for what is right, make hard decisions that others don't like, or protect yourself from human leeches, users, and abusers…people who take advantage of your generosities, or who suck the life right out of you.

Sometimes it's lonely at the top because as you grow in your career or experience success in the things you do, jealousy in others will show itself in the form of insults, attacks, or pettiness.

This is yet another reason why you have to surround yourself with strong influencers. You may have to find new friends, mentors, and coaches as you excel. This doesn't mean you dislike the old ones or that you treat them poorly. It simply means they may not be willing to take *your* journey with you. It's time to let them off the elevator on their floor and keep climbing until you reach your destination.

Moxie Minute:

It's none of your business what others think of you!
It's only your business what YOU think of you.
So how about you mind your own business!

ABOUT THE AUTHOR

Debra Fox's diverse background spans from winning Miss Rodeo Kansas, to a regional plus size print and runway modeling career, to President of the American Modeling Association, to a powerful and funny motivational speaker, and author. Today Debra still trains rodeo queens on their journey to winning state and national titles. Debra travels world-wide sharing her whimsical, no-nonsense style message to fulfill her mission of changing people's lives…personally, professionally and financially.